Achieving Peace in the Abortion War

Rachel M. MacNair, Ph.D.

Feminism & Nonviolence Studies Association
and

iUniverse, Inc.
New York Bloomington

Achieving Peace in the Abortion War

The views expressed in this work are solely those of the author and do not necessarily reflect the views of the publisher, and the publisher hereby disclaims any responsibility for them.

iUniverse books may be ordered through booksellers or by contacting:

iUniverse
1663 Liberty Drive
Bloomington, IN 47403
www.iuniverse.com
1-800-Authors (1-800-288-4677)

Because of the dynamic nature of the Internet, any Web addresses or links contained in this book may have changed since publication and may no longer be valid. The views expressed in this work are solely those of the author and do not necessarily reflect the views of the publisher, and the publisher hereby disclaims any responsibility for them.

ISBN: 978-1-4401-1325-3 (pbk)
ISBN: 978-1-4401-1326-0 (ebk)

Printed in the United States of America

iUniverse rev. date: 12/16/2008

Cover Graph: Stanley K. Henshaw & Kathryn Kost, "Trends in the Characteristics of Women Obtaining Abortions, 1974 to 2004" published by the Alan Guttmacher Institute

Contents

CHAPTER ONE
THE WELL-KEPT SECRET

Throughout history, wars have been fought, and many people have fancied themselves to have won. But preventing wars, or stopping them, has vast advantages over merely winning them. As those of us in the peace movement have worked hard to show, achieving peace involves taking everyone's thoughts and feelings and well-being seriously, especially those of the opponents.

Having gone through the exercise of studying the real-life experience of doctors and nurses involved in providing abortion in the United States, I have come to the conclusion that the abortion business is too fragile to last. In this book, I take a look at the psychology and social dynamics of performing abortions in this country. People in other countries may also find the information instructive as they apply the principles to their own situations.

THE PLUNGE

Is the abortion business in a state of decline? *Time* ran a cover story on this very point as early as May 4, 1992: "While there are about 2,500 places around the country that provide abortions – down from a high of 2,908 ten years ago – they are mostly clustered around cities, leaving broad areas of the country unserved . . . for a glimpse of the future, look at Mississippi. Three of the state's four clinics are clustered around the capital and largest city, Jackson. But their survival is threatened . . ."

Indeed, their survival was threatened. One of the major doctors who performed abortions, Thomas Tucker, had his license suspended and later revoked. The reasons for this become obvious in light of the remarks of Joy Davis, a former employee of Dr. Tucker's, which will be used throughout this book. A *New York Times* report (April 24, 1994) cited that "he was found to have kept signed prescription forms, and to have allowed workers who were not doctors to perform preliminary abortion procedures while he was absent. The eight-member State Board of Medical Licensure, whose members harshly criticized the doctor before the vote, took little more than an hour to reach its decision."

The report attributes the problems to the fact that he "travels between his clinics here and two in Alabama, performing as many as 150 abortions a week himself. The members of the board suggested that the doctor's work had suffered because of this strenuous pace."

Avoiding a strenuous pace, of course, would require more doctors performing abortions to spread the load.

At the time of the 25th anniversary of *Roe v. Wade*, it was widely reported in the media that 60% of doctors who do abortion are 65 or older. More abortion doctors are closing in on time to retire, and the new doctors to take their place are coming in very low numbers. Without an infusion of new providers, attrition alone will deal a deathly blow to the sustaining of the abortion business.

Furthermore, the number of places that provide abortions has plummeted from that figure of around 2,500 in 1992 to 1,787 by 2005 according to a 2008 report from the Alan Guttmacher Institute, research arm of Planned Parenthood.[1]

A 1993 survey of 961 abortion doctors done by "Project Choice" showed 71% claim to have witnessed an illegal abortion tragedy, and two thirds of those claim that as a major motivating factor in continuing to provide abortions.[2] That motivation is almost entirely absent now. Young doctors are much more likely to have witnessed negative medical or psychological after-effects from *legal* abortion. That might serve as a motivator to those who think they can be better and more professional than the ones who caused the problem they witnessed, but it's more likely to dampen enthusiasm for going into the field.

How have things gotten to this state? This was not how legalized abortion was supposed to work.

ODDITIES

The Washington, DC Yellow Pages has carried a one third page ad for an abortion clinic, Prince George's & Germantown Reproductive Health Services, that said, "We treat all our patients with kindness, courtesy, justice, love and respect." That had to be stated? What other kind of clinic feels it necessary to assure potential clients of this? Wouldn't it ordinarily be assumed?

In addition to the fact that it's a surgery that people attack or defend, abortion is distinguished from ordinary medical care by many oddities. It's remarkably centralized, since most of it occurs in clinics devoted to abortion as their major function. Patients ordinarily know their doctors before surgery and get follow-up care from those same doctors, yet this is unusual in abortion practice.

Health safeguards are fewer. For example, *60 Minutes* did a piece called "Suzanne Logan's Story," about health hazards at a Maryland clinic. Ms. Logan was brain-damaged and would spend the rest of her short life in a nursing home due to anesthesia complications. She died there on December 1, 1992, after the story ran. The report showed her attorney, Patrick Malone, saying:

> The anesthesia was given without any monitoring whatsoever, without an anesthesiologist present, without a nurse anesthetist present, without the normal safeguards that are part of standard modern American medical care. I've seen a lot of cases, and met a lot of doctors, and reviewed a lot of records, and I've never seen anything like this.

New York State officially ranks its heart surgeons as a consumer service. Yet New York allowed abortion doctor Abu Hayat to maim several women before prosecuting him. According to a May/June 1993 article in *Ms.* magazine entitled "Back-Alley Abortions Still Here For the Poorest Among Us," they excuse themselves on the grounds that they have inadequate resources to monitor these doctors.

These doctors deal only with women, doing something unique in female biology. Abortion is done mostly by men, exclusively on women.

Large numbers of women get abortions, and especially in New York it's one of the most common surgical procedures. Yet monitoring resources go elsewhere. The decision on where those resources go is made on some basis other than frequency or need.

A RARELY HEARD SIDE OF THE DEBATE

What explains these conditions? Why are abortion doctors so different?

Can one answer be found in the emotional impact of doing abortions on the people who do them? There is enough written and said by them to show that this is, in fact, no ordinary medical procedure. What they say shows that the peculiar nature of their work goes far beyond the fact that it gets picketed so frequently.

The reaction to the work itself is examined in an article written in the *American Medical News*, put out by the American Medical Association, which reports on a meeting of the National Abortion Federation. It says that the discussions "illuminate a rarely heard side of the abortion debate: the conflicting feelings that plague many providers . . . The notion that the nurses, doctors, counselors and others who work in the abortion field have qualms about the work they do is a well-kept secret."[3]

In a paper given by Dr. Warren Hern to the Association of Planned Parenthood Physicians, he says of his staff, "Attitudes toward the doctor were those of sympathy, wonder at how he could perform the procedure at all, and a desire to protect him from the trauma. Two felt that it must eventually damage him psychologically."[4]

In this case, he was referring to late-term abortions. But it's not ordinary for medical staff to regard surgery as a trauma. Dr. Hern is still an abortion specialist at this writing, and he gave this paper in front of other abortion specialists.

Another example comes from the article in the *American Medical News*, which states:

A New Mexico physician said he was sometimes surprised by the anger a late-term abortion can arouse in him. On the one hand, the physician said, he is angry at the woman. "But paradoxically," he added, "I have angry feelings at myself for feeling good about grasping the calvaria, for feeling good about doing a technically good procedure which destroys a fetus, kills a baby.[5]

This doctor is angry at his own patients, and he is angry at himself. Doctors are not ordinarily angry at themselves for doing their work well. The way he worded the problem gives an unmistakable clue as to why this would be, but only hints at the complexity. There seem to be some negative emotions that haven't been explored.

IS ABORTION VIOLENCE?

Defenders of abortion believe that it's a form of medicine, and should be treated like other medical practice. Opponents of abortion believe it to be killing.

If abortion as feticide is the taking of a human life, and therefore is violence, then certain psychological consequences could be expected among those who perform abortions. Human history is tragically full of instances of massive violence, and therefore we have knowledge of what those kinds of reactions might be. We will look at this in the next chapter.

If we find no such aftermath, the case that abortion is not violence at all is strengthened.

If those reactions can be found, what then? Can the United States, with its abundance of abortions, provide evidence for such a problem? Are there other negative emotions that also interfere with the smooth functioning of the practice, and account for its oddities? If so, it could help to explain a decline and predict an eventual fall.

The rest of this book will be making a case for the prediction that this has started to happen, will continue to happen, and probably can't be stopped.

CHAPTER TWO
ON THE FRONTLINE IN
THE ABORTION WAR

WHAT IS PTSD?

History has witnessed strong emotional reactions to intense trauma. Wars have been a prime cause of this problem in soldiers. During World War One, it was called "shell shock." During World War Two, it was called "battle fatigue." It's also been called "combat fatigue." Currently, the technical term for it is "Post Traumatic Stress Disorder" (PTSD).

The American Psychiatric Association officially adopted the term in 1980, soon followed by the World Health Organization; the two have different but similar definitions. The basic feature is a set of symptoms following a traumatic event outside the range of usual experience. To paraphrase these from DSM-IV, the diagnostic manual:

A. Traumatic Event
B. Re-experiencing the Trauma
    1. recurrent, intrusive recollections
    2. dreams
    3. sudden acting or feeling the event is recurring
    4. intense distress as cues that resemble the trauma
C. Numbing
    1. avoiding anything associated with the trauma
    2. avoiding things that remind about the trauma
    3. inability to recall something important about the trauma
    4. markedly diminished interest in significant activities

     5. feeling detached or estranged from others
     6. constricted affect
     7. sense of foreshortened future
D. Increased Arousal
     1. sleep problems
     2. irritability, outbursts of anger
     3. trouble concentrating
     4. hypervigilance
     5. exaggerated startle response

The idea that the trauma can be something that the individual was not victimized by but instead directly participated in causing is fairly new, but there is evidence to apply it across a wide range of acts of killing (and perhaps inflicting torture). In addition to combat veterans, there are those who carry out executions, police who shoot in the line of duty, and criminal homicide. Much evidence shows that killing may be a more severe stressor than many other kinds of trauma, and a re-do of statistics on the U.S. government data on American veterans of the war in Vietnam confirmed this as well as showing some different patterns. Those who killed were especially strong on the intrusive imagery and dreams listed under B in the above list, along with explosive outbursts of anger. Hypervigilance was also higher in those who said they had killed in Vietnam.[1] To see a good example of how that works, watch the movie *Munich* by Stephen Spielberg.

DO STUDIES SHOW THIS APPLIES TO ABORTION STAFF?

Some scholars have proposed that women who have undergone abortion have a variant of PTSD which they call Post Abortion Syndrome. Controversy rages over whether this exists or not, as will be covered in Chapter 9. Researchers have done hundreds of studies with varying outcomes.

However, incredibly little study has been done of the doctors, nurses, counselors, and other staff in abortion clinics and hospitals. Such studies exist, but they are very few and hard to find. In fact, if narrowed down to scientific studies done by researchers who don't work in the abortion field and that look at a large number of people, there are really only two.

One feature of those two studies is that they were done by people with a bias in favor of abortion availability. Yet in contrast to the varying results of the studies of post-abortion women, they both note the high prevalence of symptoms that fit under posttraumatic stress disorder.

The one published in 1974, before the term PTSD was adopted, noted that "obsessional thinking about abortion, depression, fatigue, anger, lowered self-esteem, and identity conflicts were prominent. The symptom complex was considered a 'transient reactive disorder,' similar to 'combat fatigue.'"[2]

The other one didn't mention the old term for PTSD, but did list symptoms: "Ambivalent periods were characterized by a variety of otherwise uncharacteristic feelings and behavior including withdrawal from colleagues, resistance to going to work, lack of energy, impatience with clients and an overall sense of uneasiness. Nightmares, images that could not be shaken and preoccupation were commonly reported. Also common was the deep and lonely privacy within which practitioners had grappled with their ambivalence."[3]

This may be an idea that is rarely heard, but it's actually not that controversial on those few occasions when it has been brought up in studies of groups of doctors. The case is also bolstered by observations in journals and abortion staff studying or reporting on themselves, as will be discussed below.

Abortion workers are disinclined to complain in public very often about this point. There are no definitive answers, and abortion workers themselves are entitled to those answers. There is certainly enough evidence to show that more study is warranted.

To be thorough, there is scholarship on interviews with small numbers of staff by Patricia Lunnenborg,[4] Delese Wear,[5] and Carol Joffe,[6] but these are all from sympathizers of abortion practice who are not exploring this issue. Indeed, these authors would be hostile to the suggestion of it, making their studies unhelpful to finding answers one way or the other. Additionally, there are three known autobiographical books by abortion doctors themselves: Don Sloan,[7] Suzanne Poppema,[8] and Susan Wicklund.[9] Since these are people who continued providing abortions at the time of writing, their musings provide useful insight.

UNUSUAL DISTRESS

The first thing to establish is that the "stressor," the thing causing the stress, is in fact great enough to bring on the symptoms. Things that are merely unpleasant, or mildly traumatic but not extraordinary, are not enough. Everyone has arguments and bruises. Many have divorces and broken legs. Does performing abortions bring on more than these normal stresses? Do abortion staff ever express it that way?

Sallie Tisdale was a nurse in an abortion clinic for a time, and after she left, she wrote about her experience in *Harper's* magazine: "There are weary, grim moments when I think I cannot bear another basin of bloody remains, utter another kind phrase of reassurance. . . . I prepare myself for another basin, another brief and chafing loss. 'How can you stand it?' Even the clients ask. . . I watch a woman's swollen abdomen sink to softness in a few stuttering moments and my own belly flip-flops with sorrow. . . . It is a sweet brutality we practice here, a stark and loving dispassion."[10] This woman is a nurse, so she's accustomed to ordinary medicine and all its normal squeamish details. These words suggest more stress than ordinary medicine.

The *American Medical News* looked at a workshop at the National Abortion Federation, and ran a report called "Abortion Providers Share Inner Conflicts" (July 12, 1993): "A nurse who had worked in an abortion clinic for less than a year said her most troubling moments came not in the procedure room but afterwards. Many times, she said, women who had just had abortions would lie in the recovery room and cry, 'I've just killed my baby. I've just killed my baby.' 'I don't know what to say to these women,' the nurse told the group. 'Part of me thinks, 'Maybe they're right.'"[11] Again, this isn't the kind of remark you would normally expect from a nurse.

Dr. Warren Hern, an abortion specialist, wrote a paper in which he had studied his own staff:

We have produced an unusual dilemma. A procedure is rapidly becoming recognized as the procedure of choice in late abortion, but those capable of performing or assisting with the procedure are having strong personal reservations about participating in an operation which they view as destructive and violent . . . Some part of our cultural and perhaps even biological heritage recoils at a destructive operation on a form that is similar to our own, even while we may know that the act has a positive effect for a living person. No one who has not performed this procedure can know what it is like or what it means; but having performed it, we are bewildered by the possibilities of interpretation.

We have reached a point in this particular technology where there is no possibility of denial of an act of destruction by the operator. It is before one's eyes. The sensations of dismemberment flow through the forceps like an electric current . . . The more we seem to solve the problem, the more intractable it becomes.[12]

This is a doctor who is saying outright that this is unusual and stressful.

Both nurses and the doctor were still quite firm in their belief in the need for abortion at the time they made these statements. Their idea that dealing with abortion constantly was an unusual and significant stressor, more so than ordinary medicine, didn't by any means come from opposition to abortion.

RE-EXPERIENCING

Having recurrent, intrusive recollections of the trauma is symptom B(1). An example is when Dr. Hern looked at the emotional reactions of his own staff: "Six respondents denied any preoccupation . . . outside the clinic. Several others felt that the emotional strain affected interpersonal relationships significantly or resulted in other behavior such as an obsessive need to talk about the experience."[13]

11

Another symptom is a sudden feeling that the event is recurring, which ordinarily would be imaginary. In this case, the actual event is recurring, over and over again. When the pace of abortions gets high enough that a dozen are done in less than two hours, the recurring is almost frenzied.

Susan Wicklund had a particularly nightmarish abortion of her own before she was a doctor, so part of her motivation for doing them was to see to it that women had a better experience than she did. She says that "time and again I flashed back to my own abortion. I carried those memories into every meeting."[14] The very term "flashback" is the common one for PTSD symptom B(3). She later makes it clear this wasn't just that occasion: "Every single day I worked, and with each patient I treated, I remembered that abortion."[15]

DREAMS

Dreams are so common that a mention of them, even a slight one, can be expected in almost all presentations on the subject of abortion staff's emotional reactions.

In academic literature, for example, come these cases from an editorial discussing sessions in which abortion staff are talking about their feelings. The author supports these sessions as a way to keep abortion staff doing the work:

> Their distress was typified by one nurse's dream. This involved an antique vase she had recently wished to purchase. In the dream she was stuffing a baby into the mouth of the vase. The baby was looking at her with a pleading expression. Around the vase was a white ring. She interpreted this as representing the other nurses looking upon her act with condemnation. One can clearly see the feelings of shame and guilt reflected in this dream. But more importantly, the dream shows that unconsciously the act of abortion was experienced as an act of murder. It should be noted that this nurse was strongly committed intellectually to the new

abortion law. Her reaction was typical. Regardless of one's religious or philosophic orientation, the unconscious view of abortion remains the same. This was the most significant thing that was learned as a result of these sessions.[16]

In another case, several doctors looked at the emotional impact of late-term abortions, a particular technique called the D & E procedure, on staff. They published this in the *American Journal of Obstetrics and Gynecology*:

> The two physicians who have done all the D & E procedures in our study support each other and rely on a strong sense of social conscience focused on the health and desires of the women. They feel technically competent but note strong emotional reactions during or following the procedures and occasional disquieting dreams."[17]

The same authors discussed dreams in a 1977 paper presented to the annual meeting of Planned Parenthood physicians. "As the doctor tends to take responsibility and assume guilt for the procedure, she or he may have disturbing and recurrent ruminations or dreams."[18]

The *American Medical News* reported this from the National Abortion Federation workshop: "They wonder if the fetus feels pain. They talk about the soul and where it goes. And about their dreams, in which aborted fetuses stare at them with ancient eyes and perfectly shaped hands and feet asking, 'Why? Why did you do this to me?'"[19]

A news item in the *ObGyn News* on emotional reactions to the late-term D & E procedures reports that one-fourth of the staff members reported an increase in abortion-related dreams and/or nightmares.[20]

Dr. Hern's paper recounts more dreams:

> Two respondents described dreams which they had related to the procedure. Both described dreams of vomiting fetuses along with a sense of horror. Other dreams revolved around a need to protect others from viewing fetal parts, dreaming that she herself was pregnant and needed an abortion or was having a baby. . . . In general, it appears that the more direct the physical and visual involvement (i.e.

nurses, doctor), the more stress experienced. This is evident both in conscious stress and in unconscious manifestations such as dreams. At least, both individuals who reported several significant dreams were in these roles.[14]

Former abortion doctor McArthur Hill gave his story at a pro-life conference.

> We used medications to try to stop the labor of women in premature labor so that the pregnancy could progress to term. Sometimes, the aborted babies were bigger than the premature ones which we took to the nursery. It was at this point that I began to have nightmares. Now, this nightmare is a recurring nightmare, and I'll share it with you. In my nightmares, I would deliver a healthy newborn baby. And I would take that healthy newborn baby, and I would hold it up. And I would face a jury of faceless people and ask them to tell me what to do with this baby. They were to go thumbs up or thumbs down, and if they made a thumbs down indication, then I was to drop the baby into a bucket of water which was present. I never did reach the point of dropping the baby into the bucket, because I'd always wake up at that point.[22]

Of the more common first-term abortions, Bernard Nathanson, speaking of the time when he was a pioneer in setting up abortion clinics, spoke of nightmares of a clinic doctor.

> I also recall well being cornered by the wife of one doctor at the cocktail party we gave when the Sixty-second Street clinic opened. She drew me aside and talked in a decidedly agitated manner of the increasingly frequent nightmares her husband had been having. He had confessed to her that the dreams were filled with blood and children, and that he had latterly become obsessed with the notion that some terrible justice would soon be inflicted upon his own children in payment for what he was doing.[23]

The fate of the fetus is the most common theme, but Sallie Tisdale reports another effect.

> I have fetus dreams, we all do here: dreams of abortions one after the other; of buckets of blood splashed on the walls; trees full of crawling fetuses. I dreamed that two men grabbed me and began to drag me away. 'Let's do an abortion,' they said with a sickening leer, and I began to scream, plunged into a vision of sucking, scraping pain, of being spread and torn by impartial instruments that do only what they are bidden. I woke from this dream barely able to breathe and thought of kitchen tables and coat hangers, knitting needles striped with blood, and women all alone clutching a pillow in their teeth to keep the screams from piercing the apartment-house walls. Abortion is the narrowest edge between kindness and cruelty. Done as well as it can be, it is still violence – merciful violence, like putting a suffering animal to death.[24]

The image of the men grabbing her and forcing her through pain in private parts of her body suggests that in this dream, abortion is associated with rape.

Note that only two of these cases, Nathanson and Hill, are given by people who now oppose abortion. The remaining ones are from people who still advocated for it at the time the dreams were reported.

NUMBING

Markedly diminished interest in significant activities is a symptom of numbing, as is a more constricted expression on the face. Both of those symptoms can easily be due to other things, and can be a matter of interpretation.

Feeling detached or estranged from other people may also be due to other causes, but there's also quite a bit of evidence for it coming from abortion work. In fact, the whole set-up of doing abortions in an assembly-line fashion could well be a manifestation of this. When this is done, most commonly the doctor has no contact with the patient until her legs are up in the stirrups. Unlike most of medicine, being detached from the patient is built into the system.

Nurse Sallie Tisdale talks of numbness. "There is a numbing sameness lurking in this job; the same questions, the same answers, even the same trembling tone in the voices." The numbness is not merely in the sameness, though. "Still, I've cultivated a certain disregard. It isn't negligence, but I don't always pay attention."[25]

It's in the nature of this kind of symptom that it will be reported more by the people that have left the field than by the people who are still in it. After all, it's part of the symptom to avoid noticing what's happening. Talking with those that have left does lead to a rich set of illustrations of the point, as the following shows.

Judith Fetrow worked at a clinic in San Francisco. Later, at a pro-life conference, she offered an analysis.

> When I started at Planned Parenthood, I saw two types of women working at the clinic. One group were women who had found some way to deal with the emotional and spiritual toll of working abortion. The second group were women who had closed themselves off emotionally. They were the walking wounded. You could look in their eyes, and see that they were emotionally dead.[26]

A woman who worked for a doctor in Louisiana for a few months recounted an incident in a telephone conversation.

> The one thing that sticks out in my mind the most, that really upset me the most, was that he had done an abortion, he had a fetus wrapped inside of a blue paper. He stuck it inside of a surgical glove and put another glove over it. He was standing in the hall, speaking with myself and two of his assistants. He was tossing the fetus up in the air, and catching it. Like it was a rubber ball. I just looked at him, and it's like, doctor, please. And he laughed. He says, "Nobody knows what this is."

Doctors who are accustomed to surgery which removes body parts don't generally toss those body parts around like a toy. The doctor seems to have a numbed attitude toward the fetus, an attitude of emotional anesthesia.

Luhra Tivis worked for Dr. George Tiller of Kansas, and I asked her directly about whether she saw any sign of him being detached from others.

> He had this weird thing. It was a small office, there weren't that many people there. I did all of his correspondence and everything, but if I had a certain kind of a question or procedural change, I was supposed to go through my supervisor, and she would go to him. I mean, it's ridiculous, because it was a small office. And then sometimes he would circumvent that himself, and then I'd get in trouble. So it was like he was trying to hold people off, and not have to deal with any more of the staff than he absolutely had to.

This estrangement from others can be expected to have a negative impact on the quality of the medical care. As one example, Judith Fetrow reported from her former work at a San Francisco Planned Parenthood clinic.

> The most horrifying complication that I witnessed was a woman who stopped breathing during the abortion. Dr. Michael Susman just walked out of the room when he was finished. Despite my telling him that the client was not breathing, he left me alone with her. When Dr. Susman was forced to return, we didn't even follow emergency protocol for that situation. It was a miracle that this woman didn't die."[27]

In her book, *Blood Money*, Carol Everett tells how she administered several abortion clinics in Dallas, and ended up deciding to oppose abortion. She describes a case in which the doctor telephoned and said,

The coroner called with the results of the autopsy. The cause of death was hemorrhaging from a cervical tear." I went numb. "We could have saved [her] life!" my mind screamed. We only needed to have sutured her cervix. We had everything we needed in the clinic to save [her] life, with one exception – a doctor willing to take the time to re-examine his patient to determine the cause of the bleeding. . . . Even a first-year intern would have checked for the source of such profuse bleeding.[28]

It's common, when telling these stories, to interpret this kind of callous disregard as just being sloppy, or as incompetence. That judgment may be more true in some cases and less true in others. But this fits into the pattern of being a symptom of Posttraumatic Stress Disorder.

Carol Everett's report could also actually have more to do with the symptom of having trouble concentrating, symptom D(3), rather than with estrangement from other people. The two aren't mutually exclusive, especially when these are both symptoms of the same disorder.

PREVALENCE

The studies on the question of prevalence of symptoms among abortion staff are few.

On the question of the dreams, Dr. Hern reported two out of 23 workers reported them.[30] A news item in the *ObGyn News* which focused on late-term abortions said one-fourth of the workers had them.[31] Nurse Sallie Tisdale's remark that they all had them at her clinic was probably poetic license. That symptom is clearly common enough that it should be expected to arise among a good-sized group, but not among all individuals.

There is much less data for other symptoms. A lot of those symptoms are fairly subjective, and any one of them can be caused by a lot of different things. Having a professional psychologist or psychiatrist look over individual cases with these symptoms in mind has not been done for abortion staff. The studies have noted the symptoms without saying how common the symptoms are.

However, if we just look at "negative emotions" as a whole, we can get some inkling from the academic studies. The study done in 1974, which was very soon after the country-wide legalization, reported: "A total number of sixty-six questionnaires were distributed, and forty-two were returned. . . In this particular sample, almost all professionals involved in abortion work reacted with more or less negative feelings."[32] This figure comes from an article whose concern is to ease the problem in order to make abortion workers more available.

We can't state that negative emotions can be found among all abortion workers, but this one sample, with a two-thirds response rate, and taken by people whose sympathies were with abortion work, found that it could. Whether those "negative emotions" always went far enough to be diagnosed as a stress disorder is another matter.

A major government study of veterans of the American war in Vietnam spent a remarkable amount of time in documenting the point that veterans who had been closer to the actual combat got more stress out of it than those who had not.[33] It should account for the gender difference since women were less likely to be in combat situations. The gender break-down is reversed in abortion practice, where the nurses are more likely to have negative reactions than the doctors. The analogy to abortion work would be whether those who are close to the actual procedure have more problems than those that are further away, like counselors, social workers, and receptionists. Do those that have contact with the fetal remains have more negative feelings than those who don't? The 1974 article noted that that had been concluded in previous studies, and that they found it themselves.

> Whether the professional had contact with the fetus significantly affected emotional reaction. Those staff members who had contact with the fetus reacted with much more discomfort to abortion work. Additionally, among the group of professionals who had fetus contact, there was very little variability in emotional response: All emotional reactions were unanimously extremely negative.[34]

The largest published study involved interviews with 130 abortion workers in San Francisco between January 1984 and March 1985. Unfortunately, the study didn't report on the prevalence of the symptoms, but only noted that they were widespread. They did take a look at differing definitions of what was going on in abortion work. They were not expecting to find what they found:

> Particularly striking was the fact that discomfort with abortion clients or procedures was reported by practitioners who strongly supported abortion rights and expressed strong commitment to their work. This preliminary finding suggested that even those who support a woman's right to terminate a pregnancy may be struggling with an important tension between their formal beliefs and the situated experience of their abortion work. . . .
>
> At this point in the research, the methodological decision was made to interview only practitioners who identified themselves as pro-choice and were committed to continuing their abortion work for at least six months. . . It was felt that these practitioners, most free of pre-existing anti-choice sentiments and most resistant to their potential influence, would provide rich insight into the current dilemmas and dynamics of legal abortion work.[35]

This put the sample down to 105 workers. Results showed that 77 percent bring up the theme of abortion as a destructive act, as destroying a living thing. As for murder:

> This theme was unexpected among pro-choice practitioners yet 18% of the respondents talked about involvement with abortion this way at some point in the interview. This theme tended to emerge slowly in the interviews and was always presented with obvious discomfort.[36]

That being the case, it would come up much less often on written surveys and questionnaires.

Even so, the Project Choice survey showed an interesting result along those lines. It was done from a list of 961 abortion providers, primarily just the physicians. It got a 30 percent mail-in response rate. It was not looking for PTSD symptoms specifically, and it only asked one question that really related to emotional responses to the abortion work itself. It asked whether any aspect of the abortion procedure ever caused them moral concern. As high as 38 percent responded yes.

The abortion providers were asked if they had specific symptoms, but this was put in the context of reactions to pro-life picketers, not reactions to the abortion work. About 25 percent responded that they had insomnia (sleep problems are one of the PTSD symptoms), and 23 percent reported depression. Anger (75%), nervousness (41%) and rage (41%) were also reported. Five percent reported an increase in alcohol consumption. The study was not done in such as way as to be able to separate out what the cause of those emotions was.

In talking about how abortion providers share inner conflicts, the *American Medical News* referred to abortion clinics as "America's most controversial battlegrounds" in a "political war."[37] If Posttraumatic Stress Disorder is prevalent, then the term "battleground" may be more real, less of a metaphor, than is commonly thought.

Note: for more information on killing as a trauma, see www.rachelmacnair. com/pits. *This includes a basic explanation, with links to examples from classical literature, personal stories that have been published, and an updated bibliography.*

CHAPTER THREE
DEALING WITH THE TRAUMA

It may strike many people that the obvious thing to do when faced with such stress from on-going traumatic experience is to cut out the traumatic activity, get a chance to calm down, and get some counseling. To keep going in the traumatic activity, however, requires defense mechanisms, and the world of violence has a long history of those kinds of defenses being used.

DISTANCING

The most common way to continue violence is by distancing yourself from the reality of what is happening, to isolate yourself from your horror.

One example of how this works comes from the war in Vietnam. At my college, peace activist William Sloan Coffin related a story told to him by an American veteran who had been captured. His plane was shot down, and he bailed out into a ditch. As he came out, he saw a man pointing a rifle at him, and slowly put up his arms. Though neither could speak the language of the other, the body language was clear enough, and they went marching through the jungle. At one point, the Viet Cong tripped and fell, and the gun was knocked out of his hands. The American picked up the gun, then picked up the man, handed him back his gun, and they went on as before.

At this point in the story, Coffin was startled, and asked if it were not his duty as a soldier to use the gun to shoot the man and make his escape. "Oh, it wasn't that simple," the veteran said. "I forgot to mention that there was a parade of children following. They would have run to the village to tell them, and they would have come after me and captured me, so there was no point in doing that."

It had never even occurred to him to shoot the children.

But when he was up in his airplane, bombing the villages, shooting and killing children was exactly what he was doing. From a distance, it was no problem. Close up, it was so horrifying that it wasn't even considered.

Coffin could see this right away, since he was very upset about the airplane bombing. He was using this story in speeches to show the power of distancing yourself from the horror in making it more possible to participate in the horror.

Another example comes from my college days, when we students were considering an experiment in how far people could be pushed into obeying authority. In a landmark experiment done by Stanley Milgram, an authority figure instructed the subject to give electric shocks to someone in a booth, under the pretense that this was an experiment in learning. Sound effects of human pain came from the booth in accordance with the length of the shocks. The purpose of the experiment was to see how far the authority figure could get before the subject would rebel and, as a matter of conscience, refuse to administer the shocks any more. Comparisons were then made over which people were more likely to submit to authority.

Upon looking at the numbers, the students found the high numbers who did submit, almost two thirds, discouraging. But they wanted to know more. They wanted to know about racial differences and other background differences. The experimenters had done a narrowly defined job, and it was noticeably lacking in what groups were covered. The students were hungry for more information about other groups and how they would react under the circumstances.

Then the students saw a film of the experiment.

Suddenly, the whole tone changed. No longer was there an idea that the experiment should be done on more groups. The students wondered how the experimenters dared do it at all. It was so cruel. The people who were giving the shocks were so clearly in anguish, and the pushing by the authority figure to keep giving the shocks was so clearly making them suffer, that it became obvious that the whole enterprise was unconscionable.

Such is the difference between numbers on a page and real life.

In order to keep any horror going, it helps tremendously to keep it at numbers and abstract principles on a page. The intrusion of reality must be defended against. If it can't be done literally, with distance provided by airplanes or words, then it still must be done in the mind.

Mark Twain used this point in his 1905 short story, "The War Prayer." (This is now posted in several places on the Internet). Amid the excitement and banners flying and glorious parades of the community preparing for war, the prayer at church asked God to watch over the noble young soldiers and help them crush the foe. Then an aged and mysterious stranger appeared to address the congregation, and told them what they were actually praying for.

> "Help us to drown the thunder of guns with the shrieks of their wounded, writhing in pain; help us to lay waste their humble homes with a hurricane of fire; help us to wring the hearts of their unoffending widows with unavailing grief; help us to turn them out roofless with their little children to wander unfriended the wastes of their desolated land in rags and hunger and thirst, sport of the sun-flames of summer and the icy winds of winter, broken in spirit, worn with travail, imploring Thee for the refuge of the grave and denied it – for our sakes who adore Thee, Lord, blast their hopes, blight their lives, protract their bitter pilgrimages, make heavy their steps, water their way with their tears, stain the white snow with the blood of their wounded feet! We ask it, in the spirit of love."[1]

Mark Twain ends this tale with the line showing the need for distancing to keep a war going, that it was believed this man was a lunatic since there was no sense in what he said.

LANGUAGE

The very language commonly used to describe abortion shows a certain amount of distancing. To start with, abortion defenders tend to object to being called "pro-abortion," insisting instead on being called "pro-choice." Yet abortion is the "choice" that they're talking about.

In some cases, it's gotten so that the two words are synonyms. When bemoaning the closing of the last abortion clinic in Chattanooga, one clinic worker fretted that any woman who wished to exercise her "right to choose" would have to travel to another town. But that woman only needed to do so if she chose to get an abortion. Any other choice could still be done right in town. That is, assuming that she's pregnant, and choosing what to do about that fact.

The word "choice" implies that there are several things to choose from, or at least two options. Only one choice and no choice are really the same thing. Any abortion defender who keeps insisting that abortion is necessary and many women have no choice but to abort is not really being "pro-choice." That position would imply that more options ought to be offered to those women.

In any event, modern American thought is such that whenever you say you favor something, choice is implied. Someone who is pro-gun doesn't insist that everyone have a gun, but only that the option to own one remain free. Nor do you hear howls of outrage from them at being called pro-gun. If you mean that you favor something to be mandatory, you better say that outright. Otherwise, it being voluntary would be assumed. "Pro-choice" is really just a shorthand way of saying that you think something is tolerable. Running away from a term like "pro-abortion" is a form of distancing yourself from the act.

Language describing the act itself is also full of euphemisms. "Terminating a pregnancy" sounds more benign, as does "removing the products of conception."

ABORTION DISTANCING

The practice of any kind of medicine requires a certain amount of psychological distancing. The nurse that gives shots to children has long practice in turning a deaf ear to the cries of those children. None of us blame her for it. To the contrary, she's doing essential work. She has to become hardened to it to keep her sanity. That the lay person may be repelled by a graphic depiction of an abortion doesn't really mean anything, because a lay person is likely to be repelled by the average appendectomy as well. How many of us turn away when they're showing mere shots on television? A certain amount of distancing is essential to medical work.

The difference here is the fact that people who are already medical service providers still can have reactions to the sight of abortion. In their case, it's not just the graphic nature that comes with any surgery.

Dr. Hern and Nurse Corrigan reported on their own staff. "Reactions to viewing the fetus ranged from 'I haven't looked' to shock, dismay, amazement, disgust, fear, and sadness." Since there's not normally much shock and sadness at the sight of a disembodied appendix, and people with medical training don't generally make a point of avoiding looking at surgical products, this is a clear statement of deliberate distancing.

> We discerned that the following psychological defenses were used by staff members at various times to handle the traumatic impact of the destructive part of the operation: *denial*, sometimes through literal distance from viewing the procedure itself; *projection*, as evidenced by concern or anguish for other staff members assisting with or performing the procedure; and *intellectualization*. Popularly, the latter took the form of discussing the pros and cons of performing the D & E procedure and rationalizing its value.[2]

Former abortion staffperson Joy Davis describes it this way:

> Each person that worked there had a different way of dealing with it. Dr. Tucker's assistant would look at the ultrasound the entire time she was in the room, but she

would never look down in the pan. She would never look at the tissue being removed. She never wanted to see that. She would just never take her eyes off the screen. And then I had one that would never look at the screen . . . she would never look at the tissue and never look at the screen, she just didn't want to see anything.

Nurse Sallie Tisdale describes a very conscious, deliberate distancing.

> Privately, even grudgingly, my colleagues might admit the power of abortion to provoke emotion. But they seem to prefer the broad view and disdain the telescope. Abortion is a matter of choice, privacy, control. Its uncertainty lies in specific cases: retarded women and girls too young to give consent for surgery, women who are ill or hostile or psychotic. Such common dilemmas are met with both compassion and impatience: they slow things down. We are too busy to chew over ethics. One person might discuss certain concerns, behind closed doors, or describe a particularly disturbing dream. But generally there is to be no ambivalence.[3]

Dr. Don Sloan, in a book that vigorously asserts the need for abortion to be available, also shows awareness of these tactics: "As the pregnancy advances, the idea of abortion becomes more and more repugnant to a lot of people, medical personnel included. Clinicians try to divorce themselves from the method." He goes into graphic detail and describes the need to check the body parts to make sure everything is out. "Want to do abortion? Pay the price. There is an old saying in medicine: If you want to work in the kitchen, you may have to break an egg. The stove gets hot. Prepare to get burned."[4]

COMPARTMENTALIZING

Another technique of distancing is to set the whole procedure up in compartments. A person can participate in one compartment, knowing that the other compartments are there, but ignoring them.

Luhra Tivis reports that Dr. George Tiller of Kansas, who specializes in the late-term abortions, had a similar technique.

> One of the ways he runs the clinic is, he's got nursing staff that are nurse's aides and LPNs who work in the exam rooms, where they do the sonograms, and they take blood for the blood work, and then he's got the nurse practitioner, who goes down in the basement with him. And then he's got an RN that stays at the motel overnight with them. He's got people compartmentalized. And then there's the office staff, who never have anything to do with the medical side. I was the only one on the office staff who regularly handled the medical records and typed them up. So he has people compartmentalized, so they don't all have the facts of what's going on. They just see their own little section. That way, he keeps them from getting too upset about what's going on.

Carol Everett reports something similar.

> I put (my daughter) Kelly on the telephone in the afternoon. She was thoroughly trained in how to sell an abortion. I paid her well to bring in the clients and our numbers began to rise right away. However, there was one line Kelly would not cross, even for me: she wouldn't go to the back where the killing was done.[5]

Going back to sources from abortion defenders, there is some awareness that putting things in compartments has an effect. One doctor is quoted in the book *In Necessity and Sorrow* as saying, "I think the nurses have a harder job than we do. They are the ones who see the fetus. I don't see a fetus -- maybe once a week, one -- so that there's a separation of the final product and what I do."[6]

Putting the tasks into different divisions is needed and used, but putting the responsibility into different compartments is also quite necessary as a defense. Nurse Sallie Tisdale explains, "I couldn't be here if I tried to judge each case on its merits; after all, we do over a hundred abortions a week. . . For me, the limit is allowing my clients to carry their own burden, shoulder the responsibility themselves. I shoulder the burden of trying not to judge them."[7]

There are many people involved in the whole process – counselors, nurses, doctors, social workers, clients, clients' families and partners. The responsibility can always be found to go somewhere else.

IS IT BURNOUT INSTEAD?

A lot of these symptoms could come simply from another well-known type of stress – burnout. This is, in fact, the term often used by abortion defenders who have noticed the psychological strain that abortion staff people are under. It has the strong advantage of associating no moral problem with its cause. It can be a common problem among social workers and childcare-givers, for example. Certainly activists in any social movement, such as the pro-life movement, will have noticed it as a danger.

Repetitious and monotonous work will cause burnout. Long hours and especially hours devoted to other people's problems will cause it.

This would make it logical to believe that burnout is a problem in the abortion field, and there's probably little doubt about this among knowledgeable people on all sides of the issue. Is it the explanation for those things that we have suggested result from stress after *trauma*?

For the most part, symptoms don't have labels on them to let us know their origin. Besides, the human mind is complicated, and there's no reason why there can't be many origins at the same time. But burnout can't explain the dreams. Dreams are a common symptom of post-traumatic stress, but not a common symptom of exhaustion in helping professions. Dreams have content, and come a lot closer to indicating their origin.

In any event, burnout is a much easier problem to solve, and it certainly can be solved while leaving any service organization intact. The common steps:

1) Reduce the staff-client ratio. That is, give each staff member fewer clients. Don't overload.

2) Make "times out" available. Give people a chance to withdraw from stressful situations. This is not merely short breaks for lunch or coffee, but time for staff to choose some less stressful work like paperwork or cleaning, while other staff take over the stressful responsibilities. Rotate the work so that people have a chance to get away from work that deals with people's problems. Staff can then still be serving the organization while replenishing themselves. This is called a "downshift." Vacations would also be quite helpful.

3) Limit hours of stressful work. That is, not limiting the hours of work itself, but limiting the hours of direct contact with clients. People should be aware of the limit to the number of hours anyone can work and still be productive. The negative effect of prolonged contact is increased by the severity of the client's problems.

The counselors especially are likely to be victims of burnout. If they are in a compartment away from the actual procedure, then burnout may be more likely than post-traumatic stress. Rotating their work and giving them vacations should be easy enough to do. In some cases, counselors are paid so poorly that there is high turnover in that job. In those places where low qualifications are demanded anyway, a shortage of counselors is not a daunting obstacle that the abortion business faces.

The nurses and doctors are another matter. Rotating their work and giving good vacations is more of a problem, because there's more of a shortage. Reducing the number of clients per person hardly works either. You'd have to have more doctors in order to have enough to actually give attention to each client individually.

But herein lies the big difference with most abortion clinics – the assembly-line way of doing abortions means that the doctor has remarkably little contact with the patient in the first place. Usually, that doctor only meets the patient on the table with the abortion about to be done. Whether the patient's problem is small or great makes no difference to the doctor, and very little to the nurse. Any sense of overload comes from volume of business, and perhaps from complications, but not from knowledge of individual problems.

It's certainly comforting to abortion defenders to think that burnout is the only problem, because burnout would be a much easier problem to solve than any post-trauma stress. All that's needed is to get more people involved in the field in order to spread the workload and see that no one gets overloaded.

IS IT FANTASY?

An alternative explanation has been suggested in the scholarly literature to account for the prevalence of the dreams.

Dr. Kibel explains.

> One learns about the process of conception and reproduction during preschool years. Whether it is properly explained by parents or haphazardly accumulated in a piece-meal fashion, the child inevitably mixes fact with fantasy. Unable to conceptualize the whole process in sophisticated terms, the child thinks in concrete terms. He visualized an 'egg' in 'the stomach' and believes that a formed baby develops at the outset, growing for nine months into a full size infant.[8]

Dr. Kibel believes this is the way to account for the dreams.

> As one grows one's intellectual concept of reproduction matures. But the primitive fantasies remain in the unconscious. This is universal. Therefore, even those who become intellectually committed to abortion have to contend with their own unconscious view of a fetus as a real baby. The emotional trauma observed in these nurses was a result of the psychic conflict between their intellectual commitment, on the one hand and their unconscious views, on the other. Inwardly, they experience themselves as participating in an act of murder.[9]

Is seeing the fetus as a baby just a figment of the imagination? A symbol? An oversimplification? If so, it should be easy enough to deal with.

The best way to counter a fantasy is to show the reality. With the wonders of modern technology, we are now able to show photographs of embryos and fetuses. We're able to do sonograms to show the movement and actuality of them at the very time it's occurring. A strong dose of reality should put a fantasy to rest.

Curiously, this technique seems to be counter-productive. Former abortion doctor Joseph Randall, for example, said,

> I think the greatest thing that got to us was the ultrasound. At that time, the ultrasound, or the sound wave picture which was moving, called 'real-time ultrasound,' showed the baby on TV. The baby really came alive on TV and was moving. And that picture, that picture of the baby on ultrasound bothered me more than anything else. . . . We lost two nurses. They couldn't take looking at it.[10]

I say with confidence that proposing to show the reality in order to counter this over-simplified fantasy is a practice that abortion staff will object to strenuously. They make a point of screening the information away from clients. A different remedy must be searched for, if the source of the dreams is only childish symbolism.

THE NEED

The most common response to all this is that, no matter how emotionally trying it may be on the practitioners, it is necessary for women to have access to abortion. Therefore, there must be people willing to do them. Women can't safely self-abort. If assistance is required, there must be people to give the assistance. If those people suffer strain because of it, then we need to find interventions that will help them keep at it.

We need support groups, chances to talk it out, and expressions of appreciation. We need to ease the pain of it, but we need them to tough it out in order to keep abortions available. The scholarly articles that look directly at the emotional response of abortion staff address this directly, and take this approach. As one of them put it, "With the persistent need for abortion services, and thus for willing and confident providers, a deeper understanding of the everyday experience of legal, medicalized abortion work is clearly needed."[11] We need to understand what's going on in the minds of abortion staff in order to know best how to keep them doing the job. Ambivalence needs to be resolved for the noble purpose of helping women.

If the evidence were clear-cut that women were being helped, then that technique should work. Soldiers and others throughout history have been talked into all kinds of trying circumstances on the assurance that many other people benefited from their sacrifice.

Do medical staff members in emergency rooms have the same symptoms? They would be dealing with constant trauma, and this is a real concern for all types of emergency workers. But at least they have confidence that people not only benefit from their work, but would suffer greatly without it.

With certainty that a heroic deed is being done, that a necessary service for women is being given, a person can put up with all kinds of things. With a conviction that all the problems are encountered only in a valiant effort to alleviate women's sufferings, verbalizing feelings and a chance to look at the situation and get the priorities straight would help keep emotions under control. That makes the confidence in abortion practice benefiting women a matter of great consequence.

There are problems with this, however. These will be detailed in following chapters.

CHAPTER FOUR
WHEN IDEAS DON'T FIT

COGNITIVE DISSONANCE

Up until 1957, a lot of psychological research had been done on why and how people make decisions. Much work had looked at decision making, but little had been done on the mind after decisions were carried out. Leon Festinger took an interest in this, with a special curiosity for why some people acted in ways that didn't seem exactly logical. How did they rationalize those decisions? That year, he formally introduced the theory of cognitive dissonance.

Any bit of knowledge a person has about self or environment is a "cognition" or "cognitive element." This can be a known fact or a vague concept, and everything in between.

When you have two of these cognitive elements, the relationship between the two is "consonant" if they agree with each other. Hugging someone is consonant if you are fond of that person.

But if one cognition would imply another, but the opposite is what is actually believed, if there is a contradiction, then the two elements are "dissonant" (the scholarly way of saying they're out of whack). Slapping someone you are fond of, or voting for someone you don't really believe is qualified, are examples.

Cognitions that are neither consonant nor dissonant are "irrelevant." That's important, since getting rid of dissonance doesn't necessarily mean making the ideas agree. It only means they don't disagree.

Whenever someone has any cognitions that disagree with each other, she or he experiences cognitive dissonance. This is a tension, and it motivates action. Most people try to seek relief from this instability in their thoughts. They may or may not succeed in reducing it, but most commonly, they will try. There will be some attempt to get rid of the problem by changing one element or the other to make the two either consonant or irrelevant.

Strategies for dealing with cognitive dissonance vary from person to person. But this dissonance is a strain, and people do try to get relief from it. When theorists assumed it to be a type of stress, the research seemed to confirm it.

Human beings seem to have a basic psychological need to have consistency, stability, and order in the way they see the world. When new information threatens their previous views or assumptions, they feel uneasy and resort to defensive maneuvers of one kind or another. They may "screen out" upsetting experiences. They may deny obvious facts. They may try to reinforce beliefs by making aggressive and belligerent declarations.

WHEN PROPHECY FAILS

One of the puzzles that the theory of cognitive dissonance explained was the people who set a specific date for some predicted event. When that date came and went and the event didn't happen, instead of concluding they must have been wrong, they did the opposite and preached their idea all the harder. The following is a true story and a classic in the field, but the names are fictitious.

Marian Keech had begun to receive messages in "automatic writing" from beings who said they existed in outer space and were instructing her to act as their representative to warn the people of earth of the coming cataclysm, floods on December 21. Mrs. Keech told many and by September had attracted a small following of believers. Throughout the fall months the groups held a series of meetings to discuss the lessons from outer space and to prepare themselves for salvation from cataclysm. As December 21 drew nearer some members gave up their jobs, others gave away their possessions, and nearly all made public declarations of their conviction.

Except for one interview, Mrs. Keech had confined her proselytizing to friends. During October and November, a policy of increasingly strict secrecy about the beliefs and activities of the believers had been developing. Had the group been interested in carrying their message to the world and securing new converts, they would have been presented with a priceless opportunity on December 16 when representatives of the nation's major news-reporting services converged on the Keech home. But the press received a cold, almost hostile reception.

Late on the morning of December 20, Mrs. Keech had received a message instructing the group to be ready to receive a visitor who would arrive at midnight and escort them to a parked flying saucer that would whisk them away from the flood. The group drilled carefully on the ritual responses they would make to the specific challenges of their unearthly visitor, and the passwords they would have to give in boarding the saucer.

The last ten minutes before midnight were tense ones for the group assembled in Mrs. Keech's living room. The clock chimed twelve, each stroke painfully clear in the expectant hush. The believers sat motionless.

One might have expected some visible reaction, as the minutes passed. Midnight had come and gone, and nothing had happened. The cataclysm itself was less than seven hours away. But there was no talk, nor sound of any sort. Gradually, painfully, an atmosphere of despair and confusion settled over the group. They re-examined the prediction and the accompanying messages. At one point, toward 4 A.M., Mrs. Keech broke down and cried bitterly. She knew, she sobbed, that there were some who were beginning to doubt but that the group must beam light to those who needed it most. The group seemed near dissolution.

But this atmosphere did not continue long. At about 4:45 Mrs. Keech summoned everyone to attention, announcing that she had just received a message. This message was received with enthusiasm. It was an adequate, even an elegant, explanation of the disconfirmation. The cataclysm had been called off. The little group, sitting all night long, had spread so much light that God had saved the world from destruction.

The atmosphere in the group changed abruptly and so did their behavior. Within minutes after she had read the message explaining the disconfirmation, Mrs. Keech received another message instructing her to publicize the explanation. She reached for the telephone. "Yes, this is the first time I have ever called the media. I have never had anything to tell them before, but now I feel it is urgent." The whole group could have echoed her feelings; the other members took turns telephoning. During the rest of December 21, the believers thrust themselves willingly before microphones, talked freely to reporters, and enthusiastically proselytized. In the ensuing days they made new bids for attention. Mrs. Keech made further prediction of visits by spacemen and invited newspapermen to witness the event.

Like the millennial groups of history, this one, too, reacted to disconfirmation by standing firm in their beliefs and doubling their efforts to win converts. The believers in Lake City clearly displayed the reaction to disconfirmation that the theory predicted.[1]

FACTORS IN HOW PEOPLE REACT

IMPORTANCE: Everybody holds some contradictory ideas at some times. But if the bits of knowledge that are in discord don't really matter that much, then the efforts to deal with them won't be very great either. The information that a glass of apple juice is spoiled and doesn't taste good, for example, might be dissonant with going ahead and drinking the apple juice anyway, but the tension introduced because of this may not last five minutes. Life-changing matters like buying a house or changing a job would bring in much more struggle to reduce any dissonance, and life and death matters would make the strain especially tough.

RESISTANCE TO CHANGE: How fixed the relevant ideas might be will be important in figuring out strategies for dissonance reduction. There are three sources of resistance to change:

1. How clear-cut the facts are. That the sky is blue and grass is green is pretty definite and unlikely to change. The idea that a steak tastes remarkably good is less definite. If someone spends years thinking so, but then changes an element by becoming vegetarian, it would be fairly easy to change the perception of the idea that steak tastes good.

2. How difficult it would be to change the events in question. Historical events are quite fixed, but if the air conditioner is too noisy to allow sleep, it can be turned off. Deciding that your work place is a real bummer is easier to do if you can go work somewhere else, and much harder to do if you really don't have anywhere else to go.

People will tend to focus on those things that are easiest to change. Opinions already have some ambiguity in them and are often obvious targets. Those cognitive elements that resist change the most will stay, and the efforts at reducing dissonance are usually organized around them.

3. Timing. Experiments show that attitudes tend to shift in the direction of the more recent commitment. The more recent commitment tends to have the higher resistance to change.

This resistance-to-change concept is the most important part of the theory. It's what makes the unique predictions of the theory possible. It provides an organizing point for figuring out how big the dissonance is and how it will most likely be reduced.

RESPONSIBILITY: If people have no hint that commitments might have negative consequences, then they don't cause the inconsistency, and are less likely to feel a need to explain it. But if people are responsible for deliberately doing something that has foreseeable negative consequences, then the strain to explain will be greater. If people aren't responsible for the problem, then they can merely claim they aren't accountable for its effects. But if someone is able to foresee the consequences, chooses the consequences, and brings them about anyway, personal responsibility is certainly established. The struggle to reduce dissonance rises accordingly.

SELF-ESTEEM: For a lot of people, basic self-respect is one of the cognitive elements that is most highly resistant to change. Any idea that boosts their self-esteem is more likely to be accepted and any idea that threatens it is more likely to be rejected.

SOCIAL SUPPORT: Those trying to reduce dissonance, by any strategy, are going to be able to do it better if they can find other people who agree with them. The more people that can be found who see it as reasonable to ignore the point, or find the alternative explanations plausible, the more it makes sense to the individual. An isolated believer can't withstand contrary evidence as well as a group of convinced persons can. In the absence of such support, the most determined efforts to reduce dissonance are likely to fail. But any disappointed believer can turn to others in the same movement, who have the same dissonance and the same pressures to reduce it.

STRATEGIES FOR HOW PEOPLE REACT

Cognitive dissonance is a state of conflict occurring when beliefs or assumptions are contradicted by new information. Dissonance theory holds that the conflict produces feelings of discomfort which people try to relieve by reconciling the differences, by convincing themselves they don't really exist, or by using some other defensive maneuver.

Basically, there are four ways to relieve that discomfort:

1. Dissonant ideas can be eliminated or ignored.

2. The importance of those ideas can be diminished.

3. Ideas that are agreeable can be added.

4. The importance of agreeable ideas can be magnified.

The most important factor in selecting the strategy is to figure out which idea is more resistant to change, and change the one that isn't.

If you've taken action on a belief, then the belief is more resistant than if you haven't. The more important the action, the more resistant the change. An opinion that you've expressed in a letter to the editor is harder to change than one that you've kept to yourself. An opinion you've based a career on is even less changeable.

It could also be decided that the problem is really someone else's fault, not yours. This is called scapegoating.

Finally, any belief that has support of others is going to be more convincing, and therefore resistant to change. The story of Mrs. Keech's flying saucer shows this. The reaction of that group may seem irrational, but it is well explained by this theory. When many people share a belief, or when commitment is so great that a reversal will involve severe hardship or embarrassment, the disconfirmation of the prophecy will probably be followed by increased proselytizing. People try to bolster their threatened beliefs by winning others to their cause, which increases their social support.

Some of the actions of abortion personnel may be explained by this theory. This involves their jobs, their livelihoods, and major portions of their time, so the importance of believing in the necessity of abortion availability is clear. They will have put enough of their energies into it to be resistant to change.

Since there currently is no blatant coercion to become employed in the abortion field, it is a chosen action and people will feel a certain amount of responsibility for it. Their own self-respect will be involved in any event. They have social support from other people in the clinic and from a large social movement which lobbies and rallies on their behalf.

But before we can even think of whether many actions of abortion workers are explained by this theory, we must first establish whether they do have the needed conflict in ideas.

The theme of cognitive dissonance will keep popping up for more than just the abortion providers themselves. They have many supportive groups, the pro-choice movement, the medical community, the media, courts, politicians, and their own clientele. Each group has its own viewpoints that can be analyzed with the use of this theory.

CHAPTER FIVE
WHEN ABORTION IDEAS DON'T FIT

Everyone has some mild contradictions in their thoughts that they must deal with. Abortion defenders often find such items among their opponents.

For abortion personnel, we need to look not merely at whether they might have some conflicting thoughts, but whether those are way above average. Does the actual practice of abortion differ from its defenders' ideas of how it's supposed to be? Does the knowledge of those differences cause tension in the minds of those involved?

This chapter won't discuss the arguments over whether abortion is right or wrong, whether it should be practiced or not, whether it should be legal or not. It will discuss the psychological impact of performing abortions on those who do them. Some abortion facilities aren't going to have some of the problems highlighted here. But wherever these contradictions are widespread, then the sense of cognitive dissonance is likely to be also. That means that the stress and the strategies to reduce it should be present also.

SAFETY

Volumes could be, and have been, written about the poor safety record of legal abortion. Newspapers have run major stories on scandals from Chicago to Los Angeles to Miami, and smaller newspaper articles from all over the country abound. Even the television newsmagazine *60 Minutes* has done a story on this problem, and the *Wall Street Journal* ran a summary called "Legal But Not Safe" on July 31, 1996.

Increasing safety was one of the major justifications for legalizing abortion. Getting the back alley butchers out of the business is now and always has been one of the most effective arguments of abortion defenders. That being the case, the relative safety of legal abortion is a cognitive element that is absolutely essential to anyone working in the abortion field.

The record immediately after *Roe v. Wade* did not show the back alley butchers being yanked out of business. An example from the beginning is given by Dr. Bernard Nathanson, who had been active with the National Association to Repeal Abortion Laws (NARAL) and was given the assignment of improving a New York clinic. A staffwoman is giving him a list of all the tasks he must do:

> One more thing. You got to get those doctors shaped up. I mean half of them don't even wash their hands anymore before doing an abortion, let alone scrubbing. They refuse to use masks or caps, and their moustaches are dragging into the suction machines. I swear, one of these days we're going to lose one of those guys right into the suction trap and the lab is going to tell us the tissue is pregnancy tissue and the abortion is complete.[1]

Abortion doctors such as Abu Hayat have made national headlines. The most memorable is the case of Ana Rodriguez, who was born without an arm because he had chopped it off in a failed abortion attempt. He had so many other problems that even *Ms.* magazine did an article on him, showing that the "back alley butchers" were not totally out of business.[2] In that article, Barbara Radford, head of the National Abortion Federation, which is essentially the industry trade group, was quoted as saying that there are doctors like Abu Hayat in every city.

That certainly establishes that safety problems are, in fact, widespread. You needn't take the prolifers' word for it. Abortion defenders have admitted it outright.

They will, of course, immediately point out that there are clinics that have better safety records than others, and insist that some of them are quite good.

But the question is, what kind of psychological effect does it have on those people who do work at those places with safety records less than admirable? How do people who advocate legalization for safety reasons deal with the dissonant information that safety problems are, in fact, widespread under legal abortion? Why does NAF, which is the obvious choice for watchdog over the clinics, feel little or no obligation to get these places cleaned up? Why would they leave all efforts at cleaning up the safety records of abortion clinics to the opposition? If they have confidence in their own stated views, this is puzzling.

We have two cognitive elements:

(1) legalization of abortion is necessary to make it safe for women; and

(2) there are a lot of places where abortions are performed where it's not safe for women.

It may seem logical that the best way to resolve this one is by changing number two. If watchdog efforts can be applied, that second point could be either eliminated, or at least brought down to the level that it can be accounted for by noting that nobody's perfect. Other product providers use that technique all the time.

Ignoring the second point, and deliberately sweeping it under the rug, is certainly a way of dealing with the dissonance it creates. But since abortion defenders have a strong urge for the public to believe the first point, it would seem that ignoring the second point would be an odd way of dealing with it. Yet the theory of cognitive dissonance would predict such a reaction as a possible way of dealing with it.

Judith Fetrow, a former Planned Parenthood worker, summed up the tension at a pro-life conference.

> It is extremely difficult to watch doctors lie, clinic workers cover up, and hear horrifying stories of women dragged out of clinics to die in cars on the way to the hospital without beginning to question the party line. I began to wonder if we were really caring of these women, or if we were just working for another corporation whose only interest was the

bottom line. But these are questions that one does not voice at Planned Parenthood.[3]

CHOICE

The nature of what brings women to the clinic in the first place doesn't make abortion merely one of a number of options. Nurse Sallie Tisdale reflected on her work at the abortion clinic. "We talk glibly about choice. But the choice for what? . . . Women who have the fewest choices of all exercise their right to abortion the most."[4]

A 2004 psychological study showed the following results among American women: 64% felt pressured by others to choose the abortion; 79% received no counseling on alternatives; 17% desired the pregnancy, and 39% felt emotionally attached to the pregnancy; 51% believed abortion was morally wrong (with 30% unsure); 52% felt they needed more time to make a decision; and 65% subsequently experienced multiple symptoms which they attributed to their abortions.[5] If similar figures are found in other studies, this indicates that any method that actually gives women more choices and allows them to make the decision rather than have it pushed by other people would be a method that could cut abortions dramatically.

INFORMED CONSENT

While anyone could understand people resenting the government telling them how to do their jobs, very few people would make a big fuss about it if the government were only mandating what they were already doing. If one is a professional, one would be disgusted by people who didn't meet certain standards. In the abortion field, however, the laws providing for "informed consent" by the patients were regarded as so intolerable that court cases against them were brought. For a time, they actually succeeded. In spite of the fact that, under the informed consent statute under question, the woman was only to be told of the availability of information on fetal development, and was not required to actually look at it, the Supreme Court struck down the provision with Justice Blackmun using these words: this was "not medical information that is always relevant to the woman's decision, and it may serve only to confuse and punish her and to heighten her anxiety, contrary to accepted medical practice."[6]

Even information regarding the "detrimental physical and psychological effects" and "particular medical risks" of the abortion was also struck as likely to, as Blackmun said, "compound the problem of medical attendance, increase the patient's anxiety, and intrude upon the physician's exercise of proper professional judgment."

How many people, when going in for any kind of surgery, find that having more information about it *increases* anxiety? The very admission that accurate information might increase anxiety would seem to make this kind of surgery different from others.

More importantly, the Supreme Court in this case found for women a constitutional right to ignorance. The abortion clinics demanded this, and got it for a time. This was explicitly overturned in the *Casey* decision of 1992.

Consider the bringing together of these two cognitive elements: choice, and ignorance about what is chosen. Or another set: women's ability to control their own destiny, and a patronizing attitude about what accurate information they should get.

CONSCIOUSNESS-RAISING

Deliberately keeping information from someone is in direct contradiction with the doctrine of helping women to take control of their lives. Raising consciousness is a technique that, among other things, helps to locate, and thereby helps to eradicate, any self-destructive behavior. That would make it particularly startling to find the following points, all made in clearly "pro-choice" literature.

Sallie Tisdale worked as a nurse in an abortion clinic and wrote about her experiences in *Harper's* magazine.

I describe the procedure to come, using care with my language. I don't say "pain" any more than I would say "baby." . . . It is when I am holding a plastic uterus in one hand, a suction tube in the other, moving them together in imitation of the scrubbing to come, that women ask the most secret question. I am speaking in a matter-of-fact voice about "the tissue" and "the contents" when the woman suddenly catches my eye and asks, "How big is the baby now?" These words suggest a quiet need for a definition of the boundaries being drawn. It isn't so odd, after all, that she feels relief when I describe the growing bud's bulbous shape, its miniature nature. Again I gauge, and sometimes lie a little, weaseling around its infantile features until its clinging power slackens.[7]

In an article in the *American Medical News*, "Abortion Providers Share Inner Conflicts," someone is speaking at a National Abortion Federation workshop.

"I don't think her problem is pregnancy or her problem is repeat abortions. But she has a problem. This is self-destructive behavior," another counselor said. . . For one counselor, the issue was not one of morality but risk. "Abortion is a procedure not without consequences," she said. "And so to subject yourself to risk 20 times is like mountain climbing on a peak without a rope. Twenty times is more risky than once."[8]

It could cause an "inner conflict" to realize that you are actually an enabler in self-destructive behavior. The idea of no longer being such an enabler doesn't fit with continuing to provide abortions.

One thing that doesn't change over time, however, is the kinds of questions patients ask. Questions that sometimes stump the staff. Like whether the fetus feels pain during the procedure. "This is a big concern" for both staff and patients, said a clinic employee from Massachusetts. After all, she said, "it *is* a dismembered body." Patients also sometimes ask to view the fetal remains. A Toronto physician said she didn't know "how and whether we [should] protect the patient from the reality of the procedure." She said she regularly hid the ultrasound screen.[9]

The theme of deliberate ignorance is depressingly common in the literature. An article in *ObGyn News* discussed the topic.

> Besides its use in ascertaining fetal age, sonography can be very helpful during actual abortion procedures, both as a teaching tool and as a means of enhancing safety. But sonography in connection with induced abortion may have psychological hazards. Seeing a blown-up, moving image of the embryo she is carrying can be distressing to a woman who is about to undergo an abortion, Dr. Dorfman noted. She stressed that the screen should be turned away from the patient.[10]

Another example of this comes from the textbook *Abortion Practice*:

> Vital signs should be observed regularly, and a Doppler *inaudible to the patient* should be used at intervals to determine the presence or absence of fetal heart tones. This is a controversial area, but most professionals in the field feel that it is not advisable for patients to view the products of conception, to be told the sex of the fetus, or to be informed of a multiple pregnancy.[11]

This deliberate ignorance is to be encouraged. It is noted and fostered. As Sallie Tisdale says,

> Whether the blame lies in a failed IUD, a slipped condom, or a false impression of safety, that fetus is a thing whose creation has been actively worked against. Its existence is an error. I think this is why so few women, even late in a pregnancy, will consider giving a baby up for adoption. To do so means making the fetus real – imagining it as something whole and outside oneself. The decision to terminate a pregnancy is sometimes so difficult and confounding that it creates an enormous demand for immediate action. The

decision is a rejection; the pregnancy has become something to be rid of, a condition to be ended. It is a burden, a weight, a thing separate.[12]

Thus, the element of deliberately withholding information finds its logical justification. It's what the woman wants. That this contradicts the ideals of consciousness-raising is screened out.

COUNSELING

People who are still doing abortion counseling will insist that they use non-directive techniques and have the client's best interest in mind. At a conference called "Meet the Abortion Providers," a far different picture was painted by those who had done counseling in the past. Each of the following comes from a woman who had served as an abortion counselor.

> The counseling at this particular abortion clinic was so effective that 99 out of every 100 women would go ahead and abort. So that's very effective counseling, a very important part of that abortion clinic.
>
> – Kathy Sparks

> I was trained by a professional marketing director how to sell abortions over the telephone. This man came into our clinic and he took every one of our receptionists, all of the nurses, anyone that would be on the phone, and he took us through an extensive training period where we learned how to sell abortions over the telephone. So that when the girl called, we hooked the sale. So she wouldn't go down the street and get an abortion somewhere else, and so that she wouldn't adopt out her baby, or so that she wouldn't change her mind. We were doing it to get her money. It was for the money.
>
> – Nita Whitten

We would find their weaknesses, and work on it. After the basic questions, they were told briefly about what was to happen to them after the procedure. All they were told about the procedure itself is that they would experience slight cramping, similar to menstrual cramps, and that was it.

– Debby Henry

They decided they would train me to answer the phone. So I thought they were going to tell me how they wanted the information sheet filled out, and how to keep the phone record, and this and that. But what I was handed instead was a packet of information, materials to study, on how to be a high-pressure salesperson over the phone – you know, like telemarketing. How to convince somebody to buy your product. There was nothing in the material that had anything to do with the medical profession or helping women. I was very puzzled as to why they would be doing this. I hadn't found out how lucrative it was yet. So I studied, and I tried to answer the phone the way they wanted me to, even up to the very end. I had to, because I had a very strong urge to tell women, "You don't want to come here!" But I knew that if I'd done that, he probably would have shot me or something.

– Luhra Tivis

Carol Everett made a similar point in a brochure.

When a woman calls the abortion clinic exploring her alternatives, the abortion counselor is paid to sell one product, abortion . . . The abortion counselors are paid more than they can make anywhere else and they believe in their product. In the clinics I was involved in, we didn't do any real counseling. We answered only the questions the woman asked and tried not to "rock the boat." We did not discuss any alternatives to abortion unless the woman forced us to. The counselor does try to determine the reason this woman

51

wants the abortion. Not so much to help as to use the fear
to reinforce the abortion decision.[13]

Such techniques would not be necessary if women really were
battering down the doors in eagerness to get abortions in huge numbers.
This is not the same thing as the women who, were it illegal, would
desperately seek out someone in the back alley.

If a clinic at which this form of telemarketing takes place goes out
of business, and the counselors are no longer there to draw women in,
then there are many abortions that not only won't happen but won't
be missed.

RESPECT FOR WOMEN

Any claim for women's rights must include a respect for women.
Any evidence of a lack of respect for women should introduce a feeling
of dissonance to anyone who asserts a position as being in favor of
women's rights.

Joy Davis commented on one of the doctors she believed showed
this kind of disrespect,

> I was very uncomfortable around Dr. P, so I decided
> not to work for him any longer. He invited me to go out
> to dinner with him to discuss it. I went to dinner with him
> to discuss how I felt about the way he treated his patients,
> and how he acted. He stated to me that he loved inflicting
> pain on women, which was the reason he did not use any
> medications for pain.

She mentioned another doctor from Tennessee that had told her
"that he did not have any respect for women, that he never respected a
woman, and that he certainly didn't respect women that let him come
in there and let him do an abortion on them."

Luhra Tivis reports that the person in charge of the escort service
organized by the local NOW at Dr. Tiller's clinic "stopped the escort
service because she went with him while he did some abortions,

accompanied him, and didn't like the way he treated the women. Real rough, and arrogant, and not respecting their privacy." That NOW chapter still refused to run an article against him in their local newsletter, however. There was no warning to women of what they were facing to come from them.

As another startling example of unusual medical practice, Joy Davis reports on Dr. Tucker.

> Generally at his office, we would have the patient asleep before he ever came into the room. When they were awake, he would say, 'Hi, my name is Dr. Tucker." But then, if they said anything after that, he'd slap them. If they talked during the procedure, or moved or flinched in any way, he would hit them. I've seen him hit so many patients.

This has not escaped the attention of people active in the abortion movement. For example, Marge Brerer, in a presentation on "Feminist Perspectives and Reactions," comparing RU486 and surgical abortions, contemplated the reasons a doctor might be in the business. She wondered "whether it's out of a political commitment, or whether it's for money, or whether it's a relatively sadistic way of punishing women."[14]

MEDICAL SERVICE

Some readers will have objected to our use of the words "industry" and "business" for abortion provision, on the grounds that it's a primarily a medical service. Money tends to be ample in all medical services, but the primary point is that people need the health care.

Joy Davis told a story of one of the few times the abortion clinics within Birmingham got together. "They sat down and agreed, we're going to take a half page ad [in the Yellow Pages]. That way, nobody went with a full-page ad . . . We took out the half page ad, and all the rest of them came out with full page ads."

This burst of integrity on Dr. Tucker's part didn't mean that his outfit wasn't interested in the supply and demand aspects of figuring out how to make the most money. "We always did that in Birmingham, with Summit and New Women's Health Care. We would call and act like patients to find out what they were charging for that day, and then that's what our price would be."

Abortion is one of the few medical procedures where cash is demanded before it's done.

There are also reports of performing "terminations" on people whose urine pregnancy tests came back negative. This has been reported in many of the newspaper series on scandals. Major examples include the *Miami Herald*, *Chicago Sun-Times*, and *Los Angeles Times*. People who do that can't even pretend to be providing a medical service.

Everett worked hard at the appearance of providing a medical service.

> It was always difficult to find and train telemarketers who could call themselves "counselors" while selling abortions. "We're helping women," I had to remind them constantly. Those who didn't buy my pitch quickly left.
>
> I started to believe my own rhetoric. I had to be convincing in order to persuade my telephone counselors. But each time I met with Chuck, I was quickly snapped back to reality. We were in business to make money, a lot of it.[14]

Ms. Everett was intent on the purpose of looking good on TV while actually making good money.

> I put on my PR hat and got creative. In one of our weekly meetings, I said, "Many of the women come in alleging they were raped, but they have neither reported it to the police nor gone to the hospital. I think we can get a lot of publicity if we have a press conference announcing that we will do abortions free for rape victims if they report it to the authorities. The percentage of conceptions in actual rapes is very low, and with the conditions attached, I don't

think we'll do many free abortions. But we'll get a ton of free publicity!"

Just as I had promised, we got prime-time news coverage at 6:00 P.M. and 10:00 P.M. Also, several newspapers and radio stations picked it up. I personally called on all of the 'do-gooder' organizations in town and let them know. We received lots of good, free publicity!

We never did a single free abortion for a rape victim.[16]

SEX SELECTION

Although it's not a terribly common thing in the United States, aborting a pregnancy after prenatal tests show the fetus to be of undesired gender do happen.

It's common enough to be listed as one of the inner conflicts bothering providers in the *American Medical News* article. "One of the most vexing problems providers face is their feelings about procedures done for reasons that make them – or others – uncomfortable. Sometimes it's 'sex selection' – the patient wants a boy and is carrying a girl."[17]

Such drastic gender discrimination before birth can't have a healthy impact on gender discrimination after birth. This point should bring extreme discomfort to anyone laying claim to being an advocate for women's rights.

Nurse Sallie Tisdale commented on this also.

> Always couples would abort a girl and keep a boy. . . An eighteen-year-old woman with three daughters brought her husband to the interview. He glared first at me, than at this wife, as he sank lower and lower in the chair, picking his teeth with a toothpick. He interrupted a conversation with his wife to ask if I could tell whether the baby would be a boy or a girl. I told him I could not. "Good," he replied in a slow and strangely malevolent voice, "cause if it was a boy I'd wring her neck."[18]

How is it supposed to make the woman feel to decide to abort a girl but carry a boy? What does that say to her about her own gender? Is this the woman who is boldly making decisions to guard her own autonomy? Is this helping her self-esteem? This is a form of sex discrimination, and practicing one form of sex discrimination interferes with getting rid of any others.

RACISM

Much of the advocacy for abortion availability is done by left-wing people who find racism appalling, and steadfastly neglect the racists that applaud the consequences of their advocacy.

Dr. Sloan recalls this when he was active in trying to get the New York state legislature to liberalize their abortion laws. "We had needed only a single precious vote to go our way, and one conservative upstate lawmaker had switched his vote at the last minute." A colleague said the vote had gone their way because the legislator was counting on abortion to limit the number of poor babies and keep the welfare rolls down. "'It was part people who want to put abortion into the medical code where it belongs and part racism.' . . . I hated to think that abortion reform had come out of such a philosophy, but I knew plenty of people saw abortion as a way to control the poor. . . Ending poverty would never be so simple as getting rid of poor babies. But if indeed that had been the reason behind the vote, it wouldn't have been new in history."[18]

He details Margaret Sanger's eugenics views as another example. She was the founder of Planned Parenthood. That organization routinely leaves out those racist views whenever they're praising her.

Edward Allred specializes in abortion and does it in many clinics. He was featured in a 1980 newspaper article, stating:

> Population control is too important to be stopped by some right-wing pro-life types. Take the new influx of Hispanic immigrants. Their lack of respect of democracy and social order is frightening. I hope I can do something to stem that tide; I'd set up a clinic in Mexico for free if I

could. Maybe one in Calexico would help. The survival of our society could be at stake . . . The Aid to Families With Dependent Children program is the worst boondoggle ever created. When a sullen black woman can decide to have a baby and get welfare and food stamps and become a burden to all of us it's time to stop. In parts of South Los Angeles having babies for welfare is the only industry the people have."[19]

Dr. Allred's aversion to government subsidies did not prevent him from collecting approximately three million dollars in public subsidies for performing abortions in California in 1980.

Nor is this attitude relegated to yesteryear. As recently as February 5, 2008, in a meeting of Georgia state legislators, several attested to hearing the House Speaker Glenn Richardson having on different occasions made the remarks to the effect that "if we do away with abortion we will be overrun with black babies." Wanting to give him a chance to explain himself, a meeting was set up between him and Dr. Alveda King (niece of Martin Luther King, Jr.) and Catherine Davis, both African-American women, on February 12, 2008. It was witnessed by House Majority leader Jerry Keen. They found the meeting quite unsatisfying, but the upshot is that he said he had not said the words quoted above – but that he "may have said something like that."

It's certainly true that all groups might have racists in them. You can't hold a bad apple like this against the entire group – certainly not against African-American abortion doctors. No one would say that all judges, or politicians, or celebrities, must be racist just because one of them made such remarks. The remark would be held against the individuals, not against the group to which they belong. Disciplining the individual would not be seen as weakening the group. To the contrary, it would strengthen the group by helping to purge it of the sickening reverberations of racism.

The abortion field seems to be different. Saying anything against that individual would mean admitting that the problem actually exists, and needs to be paid attention to. That's painful to admit, and doesn't fit into previously held beliefs about the noble goals of abortion provision.

Racist attitudes are not merely outrageous remarks. The consequences can be much more ominous. The following letter shows this:

> I am the mother of Belinda A. Byrd, victim of abortionists at 426 East 99th Street in Inglewood. I am also the grandmother of her three young children who are left behind and motherless. I cry every day when I think how horrible her death was. She was slashed by them and then she bled to death, taken from this world on January 27,1987. She has been stone dead for two years now, and nobody cares. I know that other young black women are now dead after abortion at that address – Cora Mae Lewis and Yvonne Tanner. Where is [the abortionist] now? Has he been stopped? Has anything happened to him because of what he did to my Belinda? Has he served jail time for any of these cruel deaths? People tell me nothing has happened, that nothing ever happens to white abortionists who leave young black women dead. I'm hurting real bad and want some justice for Belinda and all other women who go like sheep to slaughter.[20]

Though these cases were reported in the *Los Angeles Times* as abortion deaths, official records for the State of California never listed them that way.

CHAPTER SIX
MAKING THEM FIT, NO
MATTER WHAT

AVOIDING AND REPRESSION

An illustration of avoiding comes from the *ObGyn News*.

> Besides its use in ascertaining fetal age, sonography can be very helpful during actual abortion procedures, both as a teaching tool and as a means of enhancing safety. But sonography in connection with induced abortion may have psychological hazards. Seeing a blown-up, moving image of the embryo she is carrying can be distressing to a woman who is about to undergo an abortion, Dr. Dorfman noted. She recommends turning the screen away from the patient. As for staff, they need to find other ways to avoid the problem. "Staff members also may be affected by sonographic images and may need opportunities for venting their feelings and reconfirming their priorities, Dr. Dorfman said.[1]

The *American Medical News* article gives another example.

> "This may sound like repression: However, it does work for me," said a counselor from Kansas. "When I find myself identifying with the fetus, and I think the larger it gets, that's normal . . . then I think it's OK to consciously decide and remind ourselves to identify with the woman. The external criteria of viability really isn't what it's about. It's an unwanted pregnancy and that's the bottom line."[2]

Struggles on this point will generally not be public, but exceptions arise. The *American Medical News* article has several instances. A Seattle nurse talked about watching her first late-term abortion, done by dilation and evacuation method.

> "I was watching the doctor struggle with the cannula, trying to pull it out," she said. "I didn't understand what the resistance was all about. And I was very alarmed and all of a sudden the doctor pulled the cannula out and there, as I was at the woman's side, I looked down at the cannula and there was a foot sticking out. I will never forget the feeling I had in my chest as the doctor pulled that cannula out. And it almost took the breath out of me. Because the reality of this was very hard for me." The nurse said it took weeks for her to process the issue. "This sounds terribly cavalier, I suppose, but within about a month, like everything else we do after a while, it just becomes pretty routine and it has never bothered me since then."[3]

This theme comes up in the reflection of those who are no longer in the abortion business as well. When Bernard Nathanson was explaining why he changed his mind, the most important part was that, "I opened myself up to the data. When one is caught up in revolutionary fervor, one simply does not want to hear the other side and filters out evidence without realizing it."[4]

Since one of the ideas of the abortion business is that it is to serve women and give them choices, the question would naturally arise as to what they did when a pregnant woman chose to do something else. Some clinics just send them away, and others send them to agencies set up to help women through troublesome pregnancies. This offering of options is done by the people most frequently called "anti-choice." Various local groups who set up local volunteer centers, and national groups like Birthright, Care Net, and the Nurturing Network are also made up of abortion opponents.

Joy Davis's clinic did this. She was asked about this in a tape-recorded interview. She said, "We sent them to the prolifers, we knew they were going to take care of them." The next question was if it ever bothered any of them to think that they weren't the ones actually helping these women. "No. We helped them – we sent them to where they could get help." The interviewer clarified the question by asking if it ever occurred to them that they weren't helping women, but it was the prolifers that were? "When I was active in the abortion clinics, I don't know that any of us had any feelings about anything. We didn't really have a lot of feelings about the women, about the moral issues."

IRRELEVANCY

If one of the elements that is contradictory can be made unimportant, then that can take care of any tension that might otherwise arise.

An example would be the view that current numbers of population are too high, or that the current numbers of "undesirable" people are too high. There are those who are obsessed with the idea of overpopulation. Some believe in eugenics, the philosophy that certain people are burdens on society and accordingly their births should be prevented.

Many of those who believe overpopulation is the cause of most of the problems the human race now faces, also believe draconian measures may be called for. A little covering up is also justified. Limiting births becomes far more important than concerns like the safety of women, and the prevention of births is a goal worthy of the occasional dead woman. If people are less likely to be convinced to have abortions because they fear unsafe consequences, then they need to be convinced that they are safe. That doesn't make it necessary that they actually are safe, only that people think that they are. Choice, consciousness-raising, safety and respect for women all become irrelevant, which means that their conflict with a position in favor of pushing abortion would not bring on the tension of contradictions.

BELLIGERENCY AND PROSELYTIZING

The fact that some people may wish to screen out unpleasant facts or ideas that challenge their previous beliefs is hardly surprising. Very few would find this a mystery. The reason that cognitive dissonance has been widely accepted as an explanation for what would otherwise be bewildering is that it explains the irrational behavior of dogmatically insisting on something that's been proven wrong, and taking actions to reinforce the belief by getting other people to share it. This behavior can easily be counter-productive, but is done with zeal anyway. This makes sense when jettisoning any particular belief would be too painful because too much has been invested in the rightness of it.

The dynamics of slavery is an example of how this works in a social movement. When slavery started to be criticized by a handful of people, and then by larger numbers, the slaveholders could have responded by saying that was their problem and leaving it alone. But instead, they insisted on the passage of the Fugitive Slave Act of 1850, which aggressively expanded the frontiers of the slave system. It meant that Northerners now had the spectacle of manacled blacks being led back into bondage, making slavery harder to ignore. That was more effective than mere words from the abolitionists.

The slaveholders insisted on expanding the system westward into the new territories. Their biggest triumph, and their biggest downfall, was the decision of *Dred Scott v. Sandford*, in which a slaveholding majority of the Supreme Court gave slaveholders everything they wanted. This outraged many people.

A lot of non-slaveholding people who would have been happy to just leave the whole thing alone were pushed into action. The slave system was expanded. The distinction between slave states and free states was unclear when the Court insisted that the law could not treat blacks as people and that slaves, being property, could be brought up to the Northern states. Indifference wasn't possible anymore. The dynamics of the slaveholders' drive had generated an opposition.

John Noonan looked at this point at length.

> Why did the slaveholders act as if driven by the Furies to their own destruction? . . . Why did they take such risks, why did they persist beyond prudent calculation? The answer must be that in a moral question of this kind, turning on basic concepts of humanity, you cannot be content that your critics are feeble and ineffective, you cannot be content

with their practical tolerance of your activities. You want, in a sense you need, actual acceptance, open approval. If you cannot convert your critics by argument, at least by law you can make them recognize that your course is the course of the country.[5]

Abraham Lincoln recognized this in his famous speech at Cooper Institute in 1860. He was asked what would convince the slaveholders that his party had no designs on their property or the Constitution. He replied, "This, and this only: Cease to call slavery *wrong*, and join them in calling it *right*. And this must be done thoroughly – done in *acts* as well as *words*. Silence will not be tolerated – we must place ourselves avowedly with them."[6]

The sweeping nature of *Roe v. Wade* has been likened to the *Dred Scott* case before. A gradual approach of opening up abortion was working, and may have continued to work. *Roe* brought a backlash which is still going strong over three and a half decades later.

Some of the proposals that have shown that mere tolerance was not enough, but active cooperation was demanded, include an attack on "conscience clauses" that say doctors are not obligated to perform abortions.

There was an initially successful attack on "informed consent" or "right-to-know" legislation, giving a woman information that might be pertinent in her decision-making on abortion. In the *Thornburgh* decision of 1987, Justice Blackmun said that the information was not "always relevant to a woman's decision, and may serve only to confuse her, and heighten her anxiety."[7] Legally protecting people from getting information that might not be relevant is unprecedented. This established a constitutional right to ignorance for women. This case was explicitly overturned in the *Casey* decision of 1992.

In the case of *Hope v. Perales* in New York state, plaintiffs wanted the Court to add abortion to the Prenatal Care Assistance Program, or else eliminate the program. The contention was that it discriminates and takes away the constitutional rights of the women in the program if they don't have abortion. New York already funded abortions for the poor. In 1992, New York covered about 50,000 abortions at taxpayer cost of $20.5 million. This suit was not a way of getting funding that wasn't there otherwise. Arguing that a program that supplies prenatal care shouldn't even exist if it doesn't include abortion insists on everyone's active participation in abortion. The case ultimately lost.

The case of *Roe v. Wade* itself is an example. The justices found that the abortion laws of *all* fifty states were unconstitutional. Normally, the laws of a few states on some subject may be unconstitutional, but not *all* of them. In addition, the premise upon which they were so declared had never been offered by any judges before. All the states were scolded for the unconstitutionality of their laws without any warning that such a scolding was coming.

TRANSFER RESPONSIBILITY

The basic idea of saying that, no matter what the contradictions, it's someone else's fault, would have to come naturally. Since greater responsibility is one of the factors in increasing the discomfort of cognitive dissonance, the mental exercise of disclaiming responsibility would be an elementary strategy.

Just as Posttraumatic Stress Disorder may make people want to put the responsibility in a different compartment of their minds, the stress of cognitive dissonance would make people want to insist that those who are supposed to benefit are the ones who take the responsibility for it if something goes wrong.

Charlotte Taft, Dallas abortion clinic director, made this offhand remark in a recorded telephone conversation:

> For many women nowadays, they're angry that they had a choice. It's too bizarre, but it's like, if you weren't here, I wouldn't have had to make this choice. And so, instead of feeling gratitude toward the physician and a sense of [being helped] a lot of times that woman [is] in her own pain or anger, and the doctor may not get a lot of that [gratitude] these days. The woman herself may be anti-abortion.
>
> We're working real hard at this clinic to assist women in moving from a place of experiencing themselves as victim

of their decision, or of their boyfriend, to moving to a place where they see this differently . . . Victims are too annoying, you know. They don't invite your participation.

The pro-life philosophy finds no riddle in the idea that women would be angry at the presence of the clinic giving them a "choice." That clinic gives them all kinds of pressures that actually take away choices. Because that clinic is there, other people withdraw necessary support that the woman is entitled to. The father may refuse to pay child support, the employer may balk at maternity leave. Because the clinic is there, other people make remarks and even threats about that pregnancy that wouldn't make any sense if it weren't there. A 2004 study has shown that women who feel pressured by others are in the majority, almost two-thirds.[8]

This is not to argue that the women are not responsible for choosing to have abortions. But the people who pressure them into it, and the clinics that do sales on it, are also accountable. When "choice" is used as a way of saying the responsibility belongs solely to the client and not to the seller, then its meaning is different. It becomes a mental ploy.

MAKE IT A RELIGION

In extreme cases, the proselytizing on behalf of abortion can take on the form of outright religious terms. This is not common, but it happens and has been published. The *New Age Journal* carried an article entitled "Moon Times: A Meditation for Spiritual Healing from Abortion." It says, "I approach this abortion as a sacred act of compassion and letting go. Many mothers before me, in grief and with wisdom, have made holy this sacrifice."[9]

The same article says,

> It was in the moon lodge that I was finally given, at the age of thirty-eight, the kind of initiation into feminine mysteries that centuries ago were given to all young females, and I discovered there a new way of making sacred the sacrifice of abortion. . . . For those sisters who have chosen

the "sacrament" of abortion, we will make sacred the sacrifice. For those who are suffering from unhealed abortions, we will witness and comfort and confirm. . . perhaps we'll ritualize the RU-486 pill with prayers to Artemis or the Divine Mother, she who gives and takes life.[10]

The author of this article mentions that she is greatly influenced by Ginette Paris, author of the books *The Sacrament of Abortion* and *Pagan Meditations*. Paris's basic contention is that the goddess Artemis provides a role model for women seeking abortion. Artemis is well-known for demanding human sacrifice.

Paris reasons that abortion frees women to be equal to men. Without abortion, only men have the power to kill. With abortion, women have equal powers of destruction.

> Men have the right to kill and destroy, and when the massacre is called a war they are paid to do it and honored for their actions. War is sanctified, even blessed by our religious leaders. But let a woman decide to abort a fetus. . . and people are shocked. What's really shocking is that a woman has the power to make a moral judgment that involves a choice of life or death. That power has been reserved for men . . . the ancient Goddess Artemis invites us to imagine a new allocation of life and death powers between men and women, an allocation that allows men to appreciate the cost of a life and women to make decisions based on their mother-knowledge.[11]

In short, instead of achieving equality by having men rise to a higher plane of peacefulness, she advocates women lowering themselves. Instead of making war less sacred, she proposes expanding the sacredness of violence. She rightly decries a double standard, but chooses to eliminate it by embracing the violent standard of men rather than proposing a nonviolent standard for everyone.

She makes statements such as, "I believe it is time to sacrifice to Artemis the fetus to which we are not prepared to give the best."[12] She makes it clear that she is not speaking metaphorically.

MACHIAVELLIAN PERSONALITY

Another defense mechanism to having ideas that don't fit together is simply to not be bothered by the problem. While most people find a tension in the disharmony of their thinking, apparently not everyone does. We said before that "importance" was one of the factors that can make the discomfort of cognitive dissonance greater. Rather than making an attempt at reconciling conflicting ideas, some choose to deal with the problem by reducing the importance of the conflict itself.

Machiavellianism is a kind of personality which, for purposes of study, can be defined by scores on what's called the "Mach Scales." This is a series of statements which come from the Machiavellian philosophy. They are drawn from *The Prince* and *The Discourses*, works written by the 16th century Italian Niccolo Machiavelli. The Mach scales make a difference between High and Low Machiavellian people based on how much they endorse his rules of conduct. In effect, the scales distinguish between those with relative standards, such as never telling anyone the real reason for your actions unless it's useful to do so, and people with absolute standards, like those who believe honesty is the best policy in all cases.

The Machiavellian philosophy is pragmatic. It advocates behavior inconsistent with private belief when that behavior works. Telling people what they want to hear would be one example.

It could be expected that those with high scores on the Mach scales may, in general, be better able to tolerate dissonance caused by a discrepancy between behavior and attitudes. As Philip Zimbardo, who did some tentative work on verifying this, said,

> A characteristic that seems to underlie all these behaviors is the maintenance of emotional distance. High Machs do not get emotionally involved in others' behavior, or even in their own behavior. This emotional detachment or coolness leaves them free to concentrate on the cognitive, rational implications of the situation. . . Perhaps consistency has value for such subjects only to the extent that it has implications for manipulation (exploitation of others) and not for any . . . function it may normally serve for other people. . . .

> Another way of looking at dissonance in High Machs is to consider the possibility that they do not experience dissonance because of the dominant tactic in Machiavellian strategy that involves "conning" and deceiving others . . . Such an approach involves the controlled use of discrepancy and inconsistency in the service of their own gratification.[13]

The clinic directors who agreed to limit their ads to half a page in the Birmingham Yellow Pages, yet double-crossed the others and put in full-page ads, would be an example of this. They wouldn't be able to reason that they didn't lie, and they were lying to other people like themselves. They simply knew that they wanted to make more money, and they took actions in accord with that principle. All other principles were not taken into account, and therefore the conflict may have brought on little tension.

ADJUSTING

A smoker in the 1960s who first heard of the cancer effects from the surgeon general could deal with it by ignoring it, demanding more evidence, or coming out in favor of smoker's rights. It could also be dealt with by quitting smoking. This would resolve the conflict and relieve the stress caused by it. However, it could also be dealt with by a smoker making a conscious decision that smoking was important enough to be worth the risk.

The method of quitting the abortion business is available to some. Staff members who never had a real commitment to abortion, or only a mild one, and who have been there a short time, can easily quit. They also have more leeway to decide that they've changed their minds on the acceptability of abortion by virtue of having gotten more information on it than they had before. The doctor who only moonlights there can do the same, or can simply decide that he or she has other things to do. Short-term staff people have little control over the situation, and therefore little responsibility. They can escape guilty feelings more readily, or can at least seek relief from the strain of cognitive dissonance more easily.

But the doctor and staff members who've been in it awhile have greater psychological difficulty in using these techniques. Since they have made their decision after having seen all the choices, this option is less open to them.

The other technique of adjusting to the conflict is to live with both contradictory things recognized at the same time, like the smoker who decides to take the risk. In the abortion context, this is normally called "ambivalence." Those in the belligerent mode of dealing with cognitive dissonance normally deny any ambivalence, but expressions of inner conflicts are not uncommon, as shown in "Abortion Providers Share Inner Conflicts," in the *American Medical News*.

> "Ambivalence is not a dirty word," says Terry Beresford, who trains abortion counselors for Planned Parenthood and other groups. "We're not ambivalent about women's right to choose abortion. And we are not ambivalent about the need for safe, legal abortion. But abortion is not a simple-minded decision. It is a complex one. Everybody has mixed feelings."[14]

In a survey of abortion providers done by Project Choice, almost 38% responded yes when asked if any aspect of the abortion procedure ever caused them moral concern. This was a surprise to the researchers, who expected that such an admission would be rare, at least in the form of a clear-cut answer on a form sent in to strangers.

Books that take this approach include *The Ambivalence of Abortion* and *In Necessity and Sorrow: Life and Death in an Abortion Hospital*. The latter book was a series of interviews written by a Ph.D. in psychology, Magda Denes, shortly after her own abortion. She describes herself as "a pro-abortionist with a bad secular conscience."

For example, Dr. Charles Bender, age 37, (a pseudonym), said at one point in his interview, "I have no conscious conflict over killing a fetus." Then, at the end, he says, "I don't feel that any girl goes into Maxwell Plum's just because she wants to have sexual relations. She's going in there because she's seeking a relationship. We are not that liberated. The relationship is being sought, I feel, sadly, through a sexual contact. I think this has to reduce one's self-image, one's self-respect. It takes, I feel, a significant and meaningful aspect of one's life out of context. I think we're certainly living in a time of decreased human respect, of decreased human relationships, and of decreased sensitivity to killing off things." Dr. Denes herself points out the contradiction between these two statements, and her impression that he is unaware of it.[15]

Dr. Don Sloan started doing abortions when they were illegal and was still doing them when he wrote a book in which he clearly grapples with this.

> That leaves the antichoice feminists -- the "feminists for life," as if other feminists weren't. They make some interesting points, though. Their position is that choice and abortion are in reality sexist, because they absolve men of responsibility for the products of their philandering. As long as society remains permissive, boys will be boys. The only way to get them to grow up is to remove the "easy out," and make them responsible for the pregnancies they help to create. Then and only then will there be equality. Antichoice feminism has a pretty impressive list of founding mothers speaking for it. Activist Elizabeth Cady Stanton said in 1878 that abortion treats women like chattel or property. In 1869 the suffragist Susan B. Anthony urged prevention and not "execution." The woman, she said, was guilty if she committed the deed, but "thrice guilty is he who drives the woman into the crime." And in 1875 Victoria Woodhull, the first woman to run for president . . . said, 'every woman knows that if she were free, she would never . . . think of murdering [a child] before its birth.' Woodhull, a true feminist, knew even as she argued against abortion that women were not free. But it's a chicken-and-egg argument. Without freedom of choice, how can women be free?[16]

Many abortion defenders ignore the early and modern anti-abortion feminists. (For extensive documentation and original writings, see the book *ProLife Feminism: Yesterday and Today*[17]) Sloan strengthens his case by not screening it out altogether. Yet in the same chapter, he cites cases where a woman doesn't use birth control or continues having one child after another because that's what her male partner wants. As he puts it, "It's never simple. But when it comes to a choice between the man and the pregnancy, many women yield. They do what the man wants."[18] He further comments,

> It can't be pure coincidence that the three surgical procedures most frequently performed on the female patient are hysterectomy, abortion and cesarean section – all of them assaults on the uterus, the maternal end organ. Somehow, it seems that the manipulation, removal and 'cleaning' procedures that the womb is subject to arise from an attitude that it's expendable – what one feminist friend of mine calls the "'We Don't Have It You Don't Need It' school of medicine." . . . Abortion is, by almost any standards, a violent act. All surgery violates the integrity of the body; purely elective surgery seems particularly gratuitous. On the positive side, it gives women the means to decide their own fates and control their own reproductive lives. But it also puts more of the weight on women's shoulders, allowing men and society in general to literally scrape and vacuum away their responsibilities.[19]

Articles in periodicals show this pattern of ambivalence as well. The *American Medical News* broaches this topic.

> Oddly enough, many of the issues that disturb abortion foes also seem to trouble providers. Ultimately, however, they have different moral balance sheets. For providers, the bottom line is the woman's life and the particular circumstances that drive her to choose abortion. For opponents, the bottom line is what actually happens during an abortion: a human life is taken.[20]

The problem is that that the bottom line of women's welfare doesn't balance the balance sheet. It actually provides further dissonant information.

The recognition of ambivalence could, therefore, be a partial step toward reaching that reality. When deliberately ignoring and aggressively beating down the opposition are no longer available tools, a more persuasive case is made, because those methods are not really highly persuasive. Yet the reason they're used in the first place is because the need felt for them is so strong.

Naomi Wolf suggests a need to face clearly that a death occurs during an abortion, saying that pro-choice rhetoric would be more honest and therefore more effective. "Clinging to a rhetoric about abortion in which there is no life and no death, we entangle our beliefs in a series of self-delusions, fibs and evasions. And we risk becoming precisely what our critics charge us with being: callous, selfish, and casually destructive." She applies this idea to helping abortion staff.

> Pro-choicers, too, scapegoat the doctors and clinic workers. By resisting a moral framework in which to view abortion we who are pro-abortion-rights leave the doctors in the frontlines, with blood on their hands, the blood of the repeat abortions – at least 43 percent of the total; the suburban summer country-club rite-of-passage abortions; the "I don't know what came over me, it was such good Chardonnay" abortions; as well as the blood of the desperate and the unpreventable and accidental and the medically necessary and the violently conceived abortions. This is blood that the doctors and clinic workers often see clearly, and that they heroically rinse and cause to flow and rinse again. And they take all our sins, the pro-choice as well as the pro-life among us, upon themselves.
>
> And we who are pro-choice compound their isolation by declaring that that blood is not there.[21]

By no longer screening out or denying, and by no longer using belligerency as a defense mechanism, the case for "choice" is strengthened yet weakened at the same time. It's strengthened by helping to adjust to the conflicting information without resort to unhealthy ways of avoiding reality. It's weakened because those methods are no longer available to help avoid the reality.

This method of trying to adjust to the tension leaves people miserable, to the point of almost being frantic. Sallie Tisdale ends her article saying that, "Abortion . . . requires a willingness to live with conflict, fearlessness, and grief. As I close the freezer door, I imagine a world where this won't be necessary, and then return to the world where it is."[22]

Dr. Sloan echoes the sentiment. "I don't think there's anyone doing abortions who hasn't wished at some point that the situations creating the demand for them wouldn't just go away. That includes me. There have been plenty of times when I've wanted to say, 'Enough! This is more human tragedy than I want to deal with.' But that would require a different world."[23]

How long does it take to get from a strong desire for abortion to be unnecessary to a position that abortion is, in fact, unacceptable?

Adjusting is not resolving. The tension remains.

If cognitive dissonance were the only tension, that would be bad enough. But if the perception that a heroic deed is being done in the service of women is necessary to the resolution of Posttraumatic Stress Disorder, then that ambivalence will rob the abortion worker of what is needed most. Instead of having misery that's swept under the rug, the misery is out in the open.

CHAPTER SEVEN
HORRORS OF THE ILLEGAL PERIOD

In the age when performing abortion was illegal, many women faced tragedy, and the individual tales are heart-wrenching. Any public sentiment in favor of legalizing abortion finds this the most compelling argument, by far. A lot of people who are extremely uncomfortable with abortion will nevertheless oppose its ban on the idea that only medically qualified persons should be performing it, and that they therefore shouldn't be prohibited from doing so. This idea has a powerful lure on the psychology of modern abortion practice.

I would call it a legend because there is a lot of truth to it, but there's a lot of exaggeration to it as well. Most people who lived in that period didn't know anyone who had suffered from the back-alley butchers.

Dr. Bernard Nathanson was one of the founders of that National Association to Repeal Abortion Laws (NARAL), and he took a very active role in the "revolution" to legalize abortion. He later said,

> How many deaths were we talking about when abortion was illegal? In NARAL we generally emphasized the drama of the individual case, not the mass statistics, but when we spoke of the latter it was always "5,000 to 10,000 deaths a year." I confess that I knew the figures were totally false, and I suppose the others did too if they stopped to think of it. But in the "morality" of our revolution, it was a "useful" figure, widely accepted, so why go out of our way to correct it with honest statistics? . . . In 1967, with moderate A.L.I.-type [American Law Institute] laws in three states, the federal government listed only 160 deaths from illegal abortion. In the last year before the Blackmun era began, 1972, the total was only 39 deaths. Christopher Tietze estimated 1,000

> maternal deaths as the outside possibility in an average year
> before legalization; the actual total was probably closer to
> 500.[1]

Of course, a total of 500 is also unacceptable. Many more suffered who did not die. One case of a woman being needlessly injured is one too many.

However, magnifying the problem amounts to propaganda. When you're using the most effective argument you have, overstating your case is a strong temptation.

The idea that abortion is necessary because unintended pregnancy is so widespread, for example, has led to some remarkable statements. *Time* magazine claimed in its February 26, 1990 issue that, "about six million unwanted pregnancies occur in the US each year." That's certainly a lot of unwanted pregnancies. How on earth could the country cope with so huge a problem? Without abortion, so many millions of children would be growing up in pain at their unwantedness. Surely, that fact alone should show the great necessity of abortion.

One problem with this is that there were only about four million live births each year. Add that to roughly 1.6 million abortions per year at the time of the article, excluding miscarriages, and that means that you have to have each and every pregnancy be unwanted and another 400,000 imaginary pregnancies that are also unwanted in order to reach the total of six million.

The unthinking nature of the statistic is further shown by questioning where the figure comes from. There is no census for unwanted pregnancies. People who experience a surprise pregnancy rarely report its unintendedness to the proper authorities. There aren't any proper authorities to report it to. Furthermore, a pregnancy that's unwanted when it's first discovered isn't necessarily still unwanted a month later.

If they have a good case, why aren't proponents satisfied with clearly accurate statistics? This isn't intended as a remark of criticism, but as a real question.

Similar problems come with the numbers of deaths from illegal abortions. World-wide numbers of startling proportions are often given. For example, on the "CNN World Report" broadcast June 18, 1989, it was reported that 400,000 women die in Brazil each year of illegal abortions. The World Health Organization report about 40,000 deaths total for all causes for Brazilian women of child-bearing age (15-44 years). Any method used to come up with a death figure ten times greater for just one cause must have been flawed.

That same report asserted that three million abortions are performed on Brazilian teens, and that 21 of each 100 will die. Twenty-one percent of three million is 630,000. That's roughly one and a half times as many teenage abortion deaths than the number of total abortion deaths they were claiming.

WHAT CHANGED WITH LEGALITY?

In 1993, Patricia Miller published a book about illegal abortions, with a clear view to establishing how nightmarish they were. The title of the book was *The Worst of Times*. Even clearer is the description on the cover – "Illegal Abortion – Survivors, practitioners, coroners, cops, and children of women who died talk about its horrors."[2]

No points about what legal abortion is like are made, except to point out that abortions done under medical circumstances are better than those done on kitchen tables. That is the primary theme of the book, and it's an obvious point that anyone can agree with.

That does not mean, however, that the worth of legal abortion has been settled. The author of this book manages to find some of the complexities of abortion practice. There are some repugnant parts that don't have much to do with whether it's legal or not. In her fervor to show how nasty it was, she lets through some ideas that show that it is abortion itself, whatever its legal status, that is nightmarish.

> My father was an illegal abortionist . . . He was a doctor.
> He was also a womanizer and a woman hater. I don't know
> quite how all those things fit together, but I think they did.
> . . .

The one he told me about happened in 1928. He was a ship's doctor, and the patient was one of the women on the cruise. Now we think of a cruise lasting five days, but in those days they might have lasted two months. He told me that this woman asked him to do an abortion on her and that he agreed, provided she would have sex with him first. . . My father really had very little use for women. He had nothing good to say about them, and he used derogatory language.[3]

In this case, an example is given of a man being attracted to the abortion field whose attitude toward women is reprehensible. While that was not the case with all of the illegal abortionists, and is not the case with all legal ones now, it is still easy enough to find cases of it. While sex may more rarely be extracted as a price for abortion, any man with that kind of attitude will act in ways that are not in women's best interest. Legalization didn't change this.

That late-night car trip to Ohio happened many years ago, but I can see it as vividly as if it was yesterday. I sat in the front seat of this shiny new big black Chrysler Imperial with Ray in a black cashmere coat on one side of me and Lloyd, the murderer- turned-bookie, sporting an elegant camel's hair coat on the other. Lloyd drove. All the way to Ohio, the two men talked exclusively to each other, mostly about sports or gambling. I sat silent between them, feeling like I was no bigger than a candle flame in the dark. I felt almost nonexistent, like I was in some other world. The trip had a strange quality of unreality about it. . . . One of the worst things about it was that I had no control over my life. I had taken such pride in never being as stupid as my mother or my sisters, who had quite literally given control of their lives over to men, and now I was speeding west with two men, both of whom thought boxing and gambling were so important that by comparison I wasn't worth talking to. No wonder I felt like a flickering candle flame about to go out. To them, that's all I was.[4]

Here the view of the woman as something to get "taken care of," without serious consideration of her feelings or needs, is hardly something that has changed at all.

This final case comes from "Dr. Edith."

> Later in my career, the Baltimore hospitals began to establish abortion committees and to permit a doctor to do the abortion if the committee thought it was necessary to save the life of the woman. Her mental functioning could also affect her life, so sometimes psychiatrists were involved in the committee. Because I was the chief of ob-gyn, I was on the abortion committee at my hospital.
>
> Well, all these women would come and say, "If I don't end this pregnancy, I'll kill myself." As a result, that statement very quickly became one to be ignored by the committee in deciding who was entitled to an abortion. So here came this pregnant teenager. Thank goodness she wasn't my patient, but she did come before the committee. She said that she was going to kill herself. Of course that wasn't good enough, so the committee turned her down. When she discovered that she couldn't get an abortion, she tried to kill herself by taking an overdose of pills. She was in a coma for three days. When she came out of the coma and discovered that she wasn't dead, she was more determined than ever to have an abortion, so she began acting "crazy." She would scream and carry on, talk to herself, say irrational things.
>
> The committee considered her case again. The committee's decision was that because she had tried to kill herself, she might do it again if she got the opportunity. Therefore, the committee reasoned, the best way to "save her life" was to keep her confined to a psychiatric hospital until her pregnancy was over so that she could be prevented from killing herself. And that is what they did! So if you were a fake suicide threat, you didn't get an abortion, and if you were a real suicide threat, you didn't get an abortion. Something wrong with that thinking, I'd say!
>
> Actually, this teenager did beat the committee and get her abortion, as it turned out. She spent every waking minute in the psychiatric hospital trying to jump out windows, cut her wrists, bang her head against the wall, hit herself

– anything and everything. When she wasn't doing that, she was screaming and yelling. She just made it impossible for the hospital to function! After she had screamed and carried on for a week or two, making everyone else really crazy, the committee considered her case for the third time. This time the committee approved her abortion. Guess what. As soon as she had the abortion, her mental condition improved dramatically. Then, about two weeks later, she shot herself. I guess some of her "crazy stuff" was real. What happened to this young girl was tragic, and the committee didn't help any.[5]

This case is really the most shocking. Is Dr. Edith proposing the current system for this young woman? She could get her abortion right away now. She could be run through the assembly line with ease. And she could have gotten her post-abortion suicide over with much more quickly, without having bothered everybody so badly in the mean time.

People who are deeply disturbed need tender loving care. It worked out badly in this case, but how could the current system be an improvement? Mental problems require a lot of energy from professionals. It was not when she was in the hospital, but it was the point at which the professionals abandoned this young woman that the tragedy of suicide occurred.

FRONT ALLEY SOBRIETY LEVELS

The image of alcohol and drug use rampant among the abortionists of the illegal period is prominent in the horror stories that keep a strong hold on our imaginations. *The Worst of Times* had several people comment on this. "Bruce" said, "The first abortion I did was in 1961. I really don't remember much about it because I was drunk when I did it. I got drunk because I was scared. I thought it was odd that the woman didn't seem scared."[6]

"Sandra" said, "Leslie went with me to the abortionist. She called him a doctor, but I'm pretty sure he wasn't a real doctor. He didn't even wash his hands! He was filthy. I mean, he even looked dirty. He stunk of booze."[7]

When asked about alcohol and drugs, Joy Davis confirmed that Dr. Tucker had an alcohol problem.

> I'm using Dr. Tucker as a basis here, because I worked more with him than any other doctor. I can't say alcohol and drugs started once he got into the abortion industry, but I can say it got really bad once he got into the abortion industry. It would be so bad that I would come into the office some time in the morning and open up the office, and find him lying on the floor, totally nude, lying in a pool of vomit, where he had been on drugs all night, which is actually what got me started in practicing medicine without a license in the state of Alabama, because he was incapable of doing it.

When asked if this was a prevalent problem among abortion doctors as a whole, compared to other medical people, she replied,

> I used to work at a hospital. I can't tell you ever once seeing a doctor come in there just bombed out of his mind, or smelling alcohol on his breath. I can't remember ever seeing that happen, and I worked with hundreds of doctors there. And it was a daily thing in the abortion industry.

The reporting of this problem goes back to the early days of legalization. Dr. Bernard Nathanson, pioneering in abortion clinic technique, after noting the doctor who had bad dreams, said, "Another time, the wife of a second doctor, who had done at least 2,000 abortions at the place, phoned to report that her husband had developed a serious drinking problem over the past year that, in her view, was precipitated by the clinic work."[8]

Are these problems caused by the work? In some cases, it may well be the other way around. Those who have alcohol problems find that abortion clinics are much more tolerant of their behavior than other employers. Yet in other cases, the problem does come after starting abortion work.

We were able to find some people who've left the abortion business to say that they saw alcohol as a widespread problem. Actually, several said so, but they won't all be listed here. After all, every field has people in it with substance abuse problems. Maybe people who ran across that were more likely to leave the field than those who didn't. The fact is, there are no studies on how prevalent it is. Unlike some of the other emotional reactions to abortion work, where people are relieved to be able to talk about it, this is one symptom of stress that people are inclined to leave unspoken.

Many examples are found in Kansas alone. George Tiller has publicly admitted to having an alcohol problem and gone to rehabilitation services for several years. M.K. has a felony conviction for lying about his previous felony conviction for drug possession.[9] G.H. for several years was the only doctor doing the abortions at Kansas University Medical Center. On August 9, 1981, the police evacuated his neighborhood because he was "intoxicated and combative" in a house full of guns and one frightened wife and stepchild.[10] While this is only three doctors, this is limited to the state of Kansas in the early 1980s period – the entire group of abortion doctors numbered around a dozen.

There are plenty of horror stories from pre-Roe days on illegal abortionists who were stoned out of their minds or were prone to sexual assault or harassment. If those horror stories have not stopped, then perhaps it's not the legal nature of abortion that's the problem. Maybe it's the nature of abortion, period.

Substance abuse is, after all, a common thing to happen along with PTSD; it is in and of itself a post-trauma symptom. Therapists sometimes call it "self-medication" to treat the complaints.

DID WE GET RID OF THE BACK ALLEY BUTCHERS?

We did, for the most part, get rid of the garage mechanics and beauticians that dabbled in giving abortions. But according to the Alan Guttmacher Institute, the research arm of Planned Parenthood, they were in the minority. They made better stories than the doctors who did it on the side, but the great majority of abortions were, in fact, done by doctors. It's not because I think their figures are strictly reliable that I cite the Institute. We cite them because their bias would be toward making the illegal period look as bad as possible, so they are admitting that in fact most abortion providers were medical professionals.

One such doctor was Dr. Richard Mucie, D.O. He was one of the three main doctors in Kansas City, Missouri, that were known to do abortions. In 1968, a woman died from his procedure. In her corpse, her hands were shaped into claws, caked with blood. The jury gave Dr. Mucie the maximum sentence for manslaughter in the death of the woman. He got out on parole after 14 months, but he lost his medical license and set up an antique shop.

In 1973, *Roe v. Wade* came down. Because of it, Mucie went back to court and got his license back. He then literally set up shop on Main Street and heaved a sigh of relief that the police wouldn't bother him any more. But his medical skills were such that family planning clinics were never willing to refer patients to him. He stopped only when he died of an old-age-related illness.

Legalization did bring more doctors into the field. It did not, however, take any doctors out. In fact, it put doctors that had been taken out for good reason back in. The very same people who were called "back alley butchers" before were now advertising in the Yellow Pages.

Carol Everett expressed how relieved she was to find out what the aftermath was after an incident in which a woman had died in her abortion clinic.

> I couldn't believe my ears! He said what I wanted – with all my heart – to hear. Was it possible that we could kill a woman, then go on as if nothing ever happened? Was the industry that unregulated? Could H.J. get other doctors to cover for him even in the case of a woman's death? Maybe my life wasn't over.[11]

The fact that the phenomenon of less-than-competent abortionists has not stopped has been noted in publications who hold strong views in favor of abortion availability. The *Village Voice* ran "Today's Back-Alley Abortions" and "Covering up Destructive Abortions" by Nat

Hentoff.[13] *Ms.* magazine ran an article called "Back-Alley Abortions Still Here For the Poorest Among Us."[14] In the *60 Minutes* piece on Hillview in Maryland, the sister of a woman that died from a botched abortion there said, "The outcome was just like a back-alley abortion."

WHAT DID WOMEN'S RIGHTS ADVOCATES SAY BEFORE?

Back in 1870, Sarah Norton noticed the prevalence of abortion in her day and was horrified that women would die or be badly injured. She was outraged that men would be usually instigating abortions, and yet seemed to escape without criticism while the women were roundly condemned.

> The single fact that child murderers practice their profession without let or hindrance, and open infant butcheries unquestioned, establishing themselves with an impunity that is not allowed to the slaughterers of cattle, is, of itself, sufficient to prove that society makes a demand which they alone can supply.
>
> Scores of persons advertise their willingness to commit this form of murder, and with unblushing effrontery announce their names and residences in the daily papers. . . . The subject is discussed almost without restraint; circulars are distributed, recommending certain pills and potions for the very purpose, and by these means the names of these slayers of infants, and the methods by which they practice their life-destroying trade, have become familiar . . .
>
> Is there no remedy for all this ante-natal child murder? . . . Perhaps there will come a time when the man who wantonly kills a woman and her babe will be loathed and scorned as deeply as the woman is now loathed and scorned who becomes his dupe; when the sympathy of society will be with the victim rather than the victimizer; when an unmarried mother will not be despised because of her motherhood; when unchastity in men will be placed on an equality with unchastity in women, and when the right of the unborn to be born will not be denied or interfered with.[15]

This comes from *Woodhull & Claflin's Weekly*. Victoria Woodhull, editor, ran for United States president in 1872, even though women were not allowed to vote yet, and was what in those days was called a "free love advocate." In other words, these views were not the result of the prudish views of the Victorian age.

This attitude was typical of feminists in the 19th century, at the time the more stringent laws against abortion were being passed. The prevalence of abortion was viewed as a scathing indictment of the male-dominated nature of society. The conclusion of the women's rights advocates of that day were that abortion was best seen as an abuse of women.

What was the experience of the first women doctors with abortion? *The Revolution*, which was the newspaper of Susan B. Anthony and Elizabeth Cady Stanton, reports:

> Dr. Charlotte Lozier was applied to last week by a man pretending to be from South Carolina, Moran by name, as he also pretended, to procure an abortion on a very pretty young girl apparently about eighteen years old. The Dr. assured him that he had come to the wrong place for any such shameful, revolting, unnatural and unlawful purpose. She proffered to the young woman any assistance in her power to render, at the proper time, and cautioned and counseled her against the fearful act which she and her attendant proposed. The man becoming quite abusive, instead of appreciating and accepting the counsel in the spirit in which it was proffered, Dr. Lozier caused his arrest under the laws of New York for his inhuman proposition, and he was held to bail in a thousand dollars for appearance in court.
>
> It is certainly very gratifying, and must be particularly so to Dr. Lozier, to know that her conduct in the affair is so generally approved by the press and the better portion of the public sentiment, so far expressed. [T]he *Springfield Republican* says: 'May we not hope that the action of Mrs. Lozier in this case is an earnest of what may be the more general practice of physicians if called upon to commit this crime, when women have got a firmer foothold and influence in the medical profession?. . . [W]e are sure most

women physicians would lend their influence and their aid to shield their sex from the foulest wrong committed against it."[16]

For full documentation on this, see the book *ProLife Feminism: Yesterday and Today.*[17]

WHY DID WOMEN PUT UP WITH BACK-ALLEY BUTCHERS?

In *The Worst of Times*, "Detective Jack" explained something that puzzled him.

> These women were having abortions done with coat hangers, under horrible conditions, and the women I would see in hospitals were in terrible shape. Hell, alot of them were sick enough to die! But they wouldn't talk. They simply wouldn't tell who did it or where it was done. I'd plead with a woman to tell me, and she would just look away or turn her head to the wall. Even when they thought they might die, they wouldn't tell. That just made no sense to me. If one of these people who did the abortion had robbed her on the street or done any other criminal act, she would have told, real quick. But there sure was something different about this. No one talked about it, especially the women. In those days, a lot of women were losing their lives or their health as a result of abortions, but still they wouldn't talk. Why?[18]

This detective has a point that must have occurred to a lot of people. One perspective to answer his question is to point out that, in that era, cases of rape and what was called "wife-beating" were also poorly prosecuted. Women were also not inclined to take those cases to court. The defense in all those cases tended to attack the victim savagely, and it was often difficult to get prosecutors interested. In fact, beating a wife was not even a crime at the time that Susan B. Anthony was active. She got a lot of criticism for shielding a woman who had left her husband for that reason.

If rapists and wife-beaters get a wink and are ignored, then the pattern is certainly set for abortion abuses as well. In all three cases, a vigorous prosecution might follow if the woman actually died. Failing that, the amount of abuse of women that was tolerated was appalling.

Accommodating injustices against women by looking the other way when abortions are performed goes right along with looking the other way in cases of sexual and domestic abuse. Detective Jack is being logical. He's unfamiliar with the sexist pressures women were under at the time.

One doctor whose involvement in abortion predates legalization stated the case.

> A pregnant woman is in a bind. She's already in a tough spot because she's a woman in a society that is going to pay her less, value her less and generally make things harder for her than for a man. She's probably young and immature, and now she has to turn to the medical establishment, which is overwhelmingly male and full of itself. She is often embarrassed and ashamed of what she has done – as if she got pregnant all by herself. She's "made a mistake," "got into trouble," "messed up," "got caught" or any of those other clichés that young women use to describe their plight. What is the result? She will seek out whatever help she can get, and often that help is not safe. . . It seems that women will accept a low standard for abortion – shame and embarrassment get in the way of their good sense. Women all too often look on an unwanted pregnancy as "dumb," "stupid" or "How could I have let this happen?" . . . Thus women will tolerate and accept lesser standards of care for abortion, as if they didn't deserve better. They look for ways to blame themselves.[19]

This also helps explain why merely legalizing didn't get rid of the horror stories. Women who wouldn't put up with being treated certain ways by any other doctor have been known to put up with shocking behavior from abortion doctors.

Under modern circumstances, there are still a lot of women who won't put up with it, and will use the legal system to sue for malpractice. This method is cumbersome and time-consuming, but under legalization, it's the only one left to them.

Do note that all this assumes that an abortion ban applies to those performing abortions, and doesn't mean criminal charges against the women getting them. This is a safe assumption, since that's the way it was pre-*Roe* and to my knowledge no one in a responsible position in the right-to-life movement is proposing otherwise. It has been the abortionist that wanted her charged, to sabotage her testifying if she's regarded as an accomplice. There are too many post-abortion women who have sought out the post-abortion healing movement to allow for any unprecedented change in that assumption.

BANS AFTER LEGALIZATION

Two countries have instituted legal bans of abortion after a period of having abortion fairly freely available: Poland and Nicaragua. In both cases, not only did it not happen that maternal mortality went up as the back-alley argument predicts, but it actually went down.

Poland restricted abortion to those done for the more uncommon reasons in 1993, so that the number of 59,417 reported in 1990 was down to 225 in 2005.[20] It had already gone down dramatically in 1991 and then again in 1992, before settling to well under 1,000 every year after illegalization. Of course, we don't know that the registered abortions were the only ones there were, as they would stop being registered when banned. Women might also go to other countries to get them. Nevertheless, the documentation is that there was a dramatic drop in abortions.

What was the result for women and infants? For women's deaths due to pregnancy and childbirth, the number in 1990 is 70, but in 1994 it had zipped down to 36, and remained down, with the 2005 figure being 24.[21] Infanticide went down more gradually, but did go down steadily, from 53 cases in 1991 to 12 in 2005.[22] Rates of infant mortality and stillbirths also both went down dramatically.[23] Yet the dramatic downturn in abortions was not replaced by women giving birth instead. Live births went from 513,615 in 1992 steadily down each year until from 1998 on it's been steadily under 400,000 per year.[24]

Of course, there were dramatic things going on otherwise in Poland at this time, with a transition out of communism. Better economic times can well account for much of the good health news. Therefore, we couldn't relate the good health news to the abortion ban, despite the desire of many prolifers to do so by suggesting that over-all sensitivity to women in medicine becomes greater when unborn children are treated as people instead of as disposable. Nevertheless, the argument that banning abortions would mean that more women would die doesn't find any support here.

Nicaragua made abortion completely illegal in 2006 and reaffirmed this in 2007. A recent publication by Nicaragua's Ministry of Health noted that the overall maternal mortality numbers decreased by 58% in the year that abortion has been made totally illegal. There were 21 maternal deaths for 2007 compared to 50 maternal deaths the year before.

In this case, the cause is even more clear: there was an aggressive women's health-care campaign by the government. The statistics simply show the that the campaign was successful.

Many prolifers have argued that this is no coincidence – again, taking both unborn child and mother into account leads to more motivation and sensitivity to care for the mother.

Whether or not this is true, it is clear that Nicaragua is another case where banning abortion did not lead to an upsurge in maternal mortality.

Both countries have a strong Catholic background, and both have gone through major societal upheavals that account for all kinds of positive changes. Most important of all, both of them together are only a sample of two, which is far too small to base any conclusions on as to what would happen in other countries. What these two cases do show is that it's at least not always true that a ban following a legalized period would lead to a greater number of women's deaths. In the two cases where it's now been tried, it didn't.

DETERMINED WOMEN

A woman doesn't "choose" an abortion the way she chooses an ice cream cone, or a Porsche. She wants an abortion like an animal, caught in a trap, chooses to gnaw its leg off to get out of the trap.

Many abortion defenders have used this statement. Ellen Goodman used it in her column, and many grassroots activists picked it up. To their minds, it showed how utterly necessary it was that abortion be available. It showed that the horror stories of yesteryear were inevitable if abortion is not safely provided.

The statement, however, is pro-life in origin. Its author is Frederica Mathewes-Green, at that time Vice President for Communications for Feminists for Life of America. The fact that it wound its way into abortion advocacy shows that the disagreement is not about facts, but about interpretation.

If an animal wishes to gnaw off its leg to get out of a trap, is it a kindness to the animal to offer a surgical amputation instead? Anesthetic and medical instruments certainly have advantages over gnawing. But surely there's a better alternative.

The option of gently removing the trap would leave the woman much more whole. Not having a trap set for pregnant women in the first place is even better. Pregnant women and new mothers should have to settle for no less. Abortion should not be used as an excuse for leaving traps in place.

When women were being subjected to outrages from abortionists in the illegal period, the argument was put forward that legalizing the procedure would remove the scandals. This is now and always has been the most effective argument that abortion defenders have. But how long can that argument remain effective if we have tried legalization for over thirty-five years, and we find that the outrages not only don't diminish, but because more women are involved, increase?

CHAPTER EIGHT
POSITION OF MASTERY

SEXUAL MISCONDUCT

If abortion defenders are correct that abortion is necessary for women's liberation, and abortion providers should all be applauded for their efforts on behalf of women's rights, then it should follow that sexual misconduct of doctors doing abortions should be rare.

Any group may have its bad apples, and can't be blamed as a whole for it. Still, being sensitive on women's issues should mean that a collection of stories of sexual mis-use of patients should be hard to come by.

Unfortunately, not all abortion doctors themselves see it that way. Consider this, from *In Necessity and Sorrow*, which is definitely a pro-choice book:

> Basically every gynecologist doesn't like women, otherwise he couldn't work with them. He enjoys the position of mastery over them. The fact that he is the god, king, they do what he tells them, which is what he would always want women to do, because every man wants his women to be subservient to him. The patients are subservient to us, and when they rebel it's very simple: "Go to somebody else. Don't come back to me, if you're not going to take my advice." What better relationship can a man have with a woman? Besides if you fuck thirty women a day with your fingers, and in a way you do, this is a form of sexual violation. – Dr. Abraham Holtzman (a pseudonym), the chief of gynecological and obstetrical services at a major New York abortion hospital.[1]

Dr. Holtzman's view of gynecologists as a whole is unusual and inaccurate, but it speaks volumes that this abortion provider sees things that way. Certainly, not all do. But if that's a widespread attitude, then there must be something a little askew in the abortion defenders' press releases.

Bear in mind that in most cases of sexual nastiness in all fields, in all workplaces, schools, parking lots, and homes, what gets reported is the tip of the iceberg.

Here are a handful of the more prominent stories of sexual misconduct among those that have been made public. The names of the victims are removed to protect their privacy, and the names of the doctors are changed to initials in the event that any of them have improved in character and don't want to be embarrassed by past history.

Dr. N.P. is "accused of sexual battery and attempted forcible oral sodomy (both felonies)," according to the *Dallas Morning News*, June 11, 1993. The charge stems from a March 25, 1993 appointment in which a recent African immigrant alleged N.P. began trying to kiss her on the mouth, and fondling her while she lay nude on the operating table. The woman told police she awoke groggy and weak to find him fondling her and attempting to put his penis in her mouth.

N.P. has had legal problems before, and his professional conduct has been brought before the state medical license board. He has been the target of numerous civil lawsuits alleging botched abortions and was the target of sexual harassment complaints from two female employees, Oklahoma Medical Board Case #90-09-1129. The doctor has not returned from India as of the time of this writing.

Another case comes from a legal petition in a law suit:

> 6. The Defendant, R.L., while in the course and scope of his employment, performed a surgical procedure on the Plaintiff on or about June 17, 1982.

> 7. The Plaintiff returned to the Defendant on or about July 2, 1982 for a follow-up examination after the surgery.

8. During the examination, the Plaintiff was naked from the waist down and partially covered by a paper sheet on the examining table.

9. This examination was conducted out of the presence of any female nurse or assistant.

10. During the later part of the examination, the Defendant began to make sexually oriented comments to the Plaintiff and began reaching under the sheet to touch her body. The Plaintiff stated, "This is not right, please don't, please stop," and pushed his hand away on more than one occasion.

11. The Defendant began undoing the front of his trousers and told the Plaintiff to scoot down to the end of the table.

12. The Plaintiff refused and again pleaded, "Please don't do this." The Defendant placed his hands around the Plaintiff's buttocks and pulled her down toward the end of the examination table.

13. The Defendant, without the consent of and against the will of the Plaintiff, forced his penis into the vagina of the Plaintiff.[2]

Several employees testified that V.R. and his male nurse anesthetist, B.H., were frequently alone in the room with anesthetized female patients. In October, 1989, investigator Diane Robie found an envelope of photographs at V.R.'s "Today's Women" abortion clinic in Coral Gables. The photographs showed several women, undressed with their legs spread apart; the perineal area was the focus of the photographer's lens. According to the report, B.H. claimed ownership of the photos; as a result his license was placed on probation.[3]

Dr. H.S., owner of three Massachusetts abortion clinics, in 1984 was reportedly treating a young female patient at his office when he "placed his mouth on the woman's breasts for several minutes." The incident allegedly happened on two occasions. He was subsequently disciplined by the Massachusetts Board of Registration in Medicine, and lost hospital privileges in two hospitals. But he continued to practice abortions in his three clinics.[4]

The California Medical Board investigated numerous complaints of sexual misconduct against abortion doctor A.L. A patient alleged that A.L. made sexual advances and had examined her in sexually inappropriate ways. In one case, a patient accused him of sexual misconduct while performing a vaginal exam. During the exam he attempted to stimulate the woman, and subsequently engaged in intercourse against her will.[5]

In 1982, Dr. T.O. was accused of fondling a female patient's breast without medical justification. He subsequently was accused of engaging in sexual intercourse with her without her consent. This doctor, who performed abortions, was also accused of injecting patients' arms with anesthetic that caused them to become stuporous, then engaging in sexual intercourse without the permission of the woman. One woman testified to the medical board that she could not move any muscles during this ordeal, but just kept crying "What are you doing?" His medical license was revoked in November of 1989.[6]

The *Miami Herald*, in August of 1990, reported that abortion doctor P.T. was convicted of performing abortions on his former lovers without their consent. He was also investigated by the Indiana Medical Board for lewd and immoral conduct toward female patients under his care. On June 11, 1991, a jury found him guilty of two counts of battery, two counts of illegal abortion and two counts of criminal recklessness. He was sentenced on July 31, 1991 to prison.[7] In June of 1997, a Shelby County judge ordered him to pay $1.25 million damages to one of the victims who had brought suit.[8]

In 1988 Dr. T.L., owner of a clinic in Florida, was arrested on allegations that he forced an abortion on his wife. News reports indicate that T.L. came home and wanted to have sex with his wife. She was feeling sick from the pregnancy and declined. According to his wife, he then handcuffed her hands behind her back and forced her into the bathroom of their home, secured her with a medical apparatus to the floor and used tape. After the incomplete abortion, which sent her to the hospital, the wife called the police. The criminal charges were dropped by the wife because, she said, she was too ill to testify, but the incident is on file as a matter of public record with the state medical board. Medical board officials did not pursue the matter, and the doctor continued operating.[8]

In 1987, the Tamarac, FL police department began an investigation into allegations of sexual assault by abortion doctor J.G. He was employed by the University Women's Center abortion clinic. He was never tried on charges developed during investigations, because he died in a traffic accident prior to trial. Several cases were dismissed after his death.[9]

The Clarion Ledger in Jackson, Mississippi offers another example. "A doctor who works at a Jackson abortion clinic was arrested Friday on charges he mailed videotapes of minors involved in sexually explicit conduct to a person in Madison, Wisconsin . . . The tapes contained scenes of minors as young as four engaged in sexual conduct with adult males and females." M.C. "faces not less than 20 years and up to life imprisonment under a charge of sexually exploiting children."[10] He drew a 13 month prison sentence and a $6,000 fine.[11]

In 1983, Dr. N. G.'s medical license in Kentucky was revoked following his conviction on four counts of unlawful sexual transaction with a minor (a 14 year old neighbor). In 1989, he was performing abortions in Florida, but had his license revoked. He moved to Ohio, and practiced until the Ohio Medical Board learned of his history, and won an appeal to upholding his revocation in February of 1993.[12]

Dr. R.T. had his Florida medical license suspended following an abortion-related death of a patient. In 1985, after moving to Michigan, his medical license was revoked after his conviction of First Degree criminal sexual assault and second decree criminal sexual conduct. He had forcibly transported a six year old girl in his car against her will. He admitted exposing himself to the girl and placing her hand on his penis. He also lifted the child's undergarment to expose her vulva. He released the girl when she began to cry. He was also cited for masturbating in his car outside a high school where young girls were exiting. He was released from prison on January 3, 1990, and his parole ended on August 15, 1991. He was licensed to practice by the state of New York in August of 1992.[13]

In 2003, a jury found B.F. guilty on charges of 22 counts of sexual abuse out of 67 counts alleged. Over 100 women had complained once a first case became public in September 2001; that is, one public case brought on an onrush of women who had not complained until they knew they were not alone. These were cases that occurred during medical examination, and one staff member had quit over observing his practices. B.F. performed about 20% of the abortions done in Arizona, having done around 30,000 in his career, and had served as a prominent media spokesperson for the cause. He was sentenced to nearly 35 years and told to register as a sex offender with life-time probation.

Some of the thinking behind sexual abuse is startlingly illustrated by the case of a student nurse, who filed a charge of rape against Dr. J.F. This is her affidavit.

> It was my job to assist the doctors. I scrubbed with Dr. F. While scrubbing at the sink, Dr. F. kidded me about my size. He said that birth control pills would put some weight on me. He asked me if I was on them. I didn't need to be. He then said he would give me a prescription. I assisted him with the delivery and after cleaning the instruments, I went out to the nurses' station.
>
> [Later that day] Just as I was leaving the lounge, Dr. F. was, as it appeared, on his way to the doctors' lounge. He said, "come here," and started walking down the hall. I said, "I'm not going in there." He then said, "that's not where we're going." I then asked, "where are we going?' Then he said, "you never ask a doctor where he's going." Then he grabbed my arm and pulled me down the stairs. . . . Still holding on to me, he took me down the hall on the left as you leave the stairs. He pulled me into a dark room on the left. Once in the room, I saw it was still under construction. The halls were completely empty. I didn't see anyone when I came onto the floor or when I left.
>
> Thinking I could reason with him, I begged him to let me go. But he wouldn't listen. He didn't say anything and kept trying to kiss me. I kept pulling away and he kept tightening his grip on my arms. Then he said, "we've got to work out something." I said, "no!" He seemed to really be mad and I pulled away to head for the door and he jerked

my arm. I knew now he had no intentions of letting me go. I was afraid to scream. I feared for my life. He then began pulling down my scrub suit pants and I fought him, but he kept one of my arms behind my back and he was able to get them down. I struggled with him, but he kept both my arms in his grip. I wasn't strong enough to get away and he knew it. He raped me. He then backed away from me and as I stood there crying, he said, "I knew there wouldn't be another time or place."[14]

RESPONDING

The usual response by official abortion spokespersons when these stories arise is to say that they are outrageous, but isolated incidents. For example, Jennifer Jackson, in 1989 President of the Massachusetts chapter of the National Organization for Women, was asked about the H.S. case above. "NOW is appalled to learn of any doctors engaged in the sexual exploitation of women. But this is only one doctor and one incident. Others working to provide safe abortions should not be tainted by it."[15]

You would expect the Massachusetts NOW chapter to not merely say how appalled they were by H.S.'s conduct, but also by the fact that he continued to do abortions long afterward. You would not normally expect real women's rights advocates to follow any statement of being appalled with an immediate disclaimer for the field as a whole, to temper an expression of outrage with an assertion that other people aren't as bad as this one.

In the case of B.F., the response was even worse: the spokesperson for the Arizona chapter of the National Organization for Women, familiar with the case, assured people that the women were lying, and this was due to an anti-abortion conspiracy. How over 100 women of sufficient pro-choice philosophy to go to an abortion provider, many if not most of whom were in fact getting abortions, along with several former employees of the clinic, were talked into making the allegations was not clearly explained. Advocates in NOW are not normally inclined to take the side of the accused in sexual abuse cases, outside the context of the accused being an abortion provider.

Those who hold to anti-abortion theory find no mystery in the numbers of cases that have come to light. The assembly-line clean-up of women, which makes them more available as re-usable sex machines, would be expected to attract practitioners of that mentality.

Can these problems be cleaned up? Surely the bad apples can be gotten rid of, leaving the clinics safer. It would make perfect sense for abortion "watchdog" groups to be active in ensuring that women get only the best and most sensitive of care. If it were in fact rare, then getting rid of it should not be that great a task, and would also be of intense interest to any genuine women's rights advocates.

Abortion clinics occasionally unleash the temptations of sexual conquest already so common in our culture. With the closed environment that abortion clinics operate in, and with the hidden nature of most sexual domination wherever it may be, it's not possible to say how much is going on. Nor can we ever know how the legal situation compares with the previous illegal one.

But we do know that the response to those cases that do come to light is remarkable. It shows a rather dangerous attitude when you consider the urgent need to get rid of this misbehavior in our society as a whole. We need to give support to women who are victimized by it, rather than worrying about the public relations damage any disclosures might do.

AND THE REST OF US?

Most of the above cases deal with abuse of patients. A couple deal with forced abortion on wives and lovers, and three deal with sexual abuse of children, rather than with abortion practice directly.

The last case, the rape of a nurse, is totally outside of the context of abortion. The events alleged happened in a hospital doing deliveries. We know that Dr. J.F. did abortions because of other legal troubles he had, not because of this case. But this case brings up one final important point – the effect that ready access to abortion has on rape and other sexual assaults in the entire society.

Though there was never a conviction in this case because Dr. J.F. died in a car accident before trial, and we can't say that the actual events are as stated, his statements to her do serve as an illustration of how abortion can serve the sexually exploitative, and thereby increases how often sexual exploitation is committed.

According to her affidavit, the perpetrator was concerned about the victim's birth control arrangements. He seemed to be under the impression that she was *obligated* to be sexually available to him. To him, a "woman's right to choose" came to serve a "man's right to use." And the "woman's right to choose" to have an abortion makes it unnecessary for her to have a right to choose whether or not to have sex when he wanted it. She could control her own body after he was done with it.

The massive amount of rape and sexual abuse in America has been called a war on women. Most men are just as outraged as women are about it. Literal wars with soldiers and lines of command have seen rape as a common practice.[16] If sexual assaults against women are part of the abortion war, this is clearly a part that no one on any advocacy side of the abortion debate had in mind. It should be uncovered so that it can be rooted out.

STRESS

Does this problem relate to the two forms of stress we have been covering – post-trauma and cognitive dissonance? The relationship of sex drive to trauma in combat has been observed but not completely studied, giving clues but still requiring further investigation. As for dissonance, those doctors engaged in both abortion and sexual exploitation or outright rape have generally worked out the problem of consistency between the two in their minds. For women's rights advocates, however, this provides another conundrum that needs to be mentally processed. Avoidance is generally the preferred technique.

CHAPTER NINE
POST-ABORTION WOMEN

INGROUP-OUTGROUP

The psychology of abortion staff hasn't been studied or discussed nearly as much as whether or not the women getting abortions are traumatized. Hundreds of studies have been done, and debate on the point is quite heated. Post-abortion women who make that claim are a major constituency group of the pro-life movement; like combat veterans of a war who oppose that war, they are among the most effective in impacting public opinion. They also help talk other women out of going through the same experience. Nevertheless, before we get into that, we're going to discuss ingroup-outgroup dynamics, and then explain why.

The ingroup is the group a person is in, and identifies with. The outgroup is a group a person considers to be *other* people. Social psychologists have noted several things about this. Stereotypes, of course, are aimed at an outgroup. But there is much more to it than that.

People can easily see the differences between individuals in their own ingroups. You'll trust Chris to be punctual but not to handle money; you'll trust Terry with your money but not to be there with it on time.

There is a tendency for these understandings of individual differences to drop when a person looks at individuals in an outgroup. The less known the outgroup is, the greater is what is called the "outgroup homogeneity effect." People in an outgroup are distant, so differences get blurred. The more distant the group, the greater the blurring. It's where the idea comes from, in referring to another racial group, "they all look alike." They don't look alike to each other, of course, and they also no longer do when they become friends and are no longer an outgroup.

Once people are seen as members of a outgroup rather than as individuals, then they also can be seen as not quite being human. This is one of the things that can cause violence, especially if de-humanizing goes to the length of demonizing. But it can also cause people to do more minor rule-breaking things, as will be covered below, when they see people as being in an outgroup.

The ingroup also provides pressures for conformity. In a famous series of experiments in the 1950s, Solomon Asch had people answering questions involving judging the length of lines in a task that very few would get wrong when simply asked. Yet when put in a group with a bunch of confederates of the experimenter, in which the confederates would all unanimously give the same wrong answer, people had a strong tendency to also give that wrong answer. Experimenters found that one or two confederates wouldn't have that effect – it needed to be three or more. The confederates needed to be unanimous on the same wrong answer; just one confederate giving a different wrong answer made the person more likely to give the obvious correct answer.

Some people really thought they saw the wrong answer because with so many people telling them what it was, they thought that's what it must be. Other people knew better but didn't want to have a conflict with the rest of the group. Length of lines is hardly the kind of thing to go to the mat for. Either way, the behavior is the same: people conformed with the group rather than the evidence of their own eyes.

APA TASK FORCE ON MENTAL HEALTH AND ABORTION

In the spring of 2006, a Task Force was formed by the American Psychological Association (APA) to take a look at all the studies done on the psychological aftermath to women following abortion. Despite its title, they were uninterested in the impact on men, other family members, or abortion staff.

The members were hand-picked without any input from outside the group. Three of the six had strong views in favor of abortion availability, and the other three had nothing easily findable on the topic.

The APA had done a previous such task force in 1989, when the number of studies was far fewer. It had concluded that the majority of post-abortion women suffered no mental problems due to that experience. The same is true of combat veterans, a group no one denies as having many suffering post-experience trauma, so the wording of the conclusion is political rather than interested in possible therapy needs. The later task force included members from the previous one, but no skeptics of that previous position.

Objections were raised that the task force was not balanced as one would expect of scientific endeavor, including a letter sent to every APA Council member by the group Consistent Life. All objections were either ignored or met with assurances that it would be the science that would decide the conclusion, not the political opinion of participants.

Part of the science is that they would have reviewers of differing views, and that they did do. That is, once the original report was written by the task force, they would get people with expertise to read it and give them feedback on how well they did and suggestions for how they could improve it. There were 20 reviewers, a respectable number, and I (Rachel MacNair) was one. Priscilla Coleman was another who has done several studies in this area. David Fergusson of New Zealand also served; he had done a major large study. David is self-described as an "atheist pro-choicer," and his opinion about the quality of the science was roughly the same as mine and Priscilla's, so it isn't merely a pro-lifer's bias.

I got the original November 2 2007 report and spent 30-40 hours giving them careful line-by-line commentary. Once I got the March 6 2008 revised version, I saw they had re-organized it, and based a more clearly worded conclusion on an entirely different approach. Rather than including my alternative perspectives for balance on several previous arguments they made, they had simply left out those arguments. The new version never went through the process of expert review.

There was, at least, one major improvement: the short section on the abortion-as-trauma "conceptual framework" had dropped the grotesque caricature of pro-lifers and instead offered an explanation that left the reader no longer puzzled as to why anybody might think abortion was traumatic. Still, it was shorter and simpler than the other conceptual frameworks, showing the outgroup homogeneity effect. Additionally, unlike the others, it included an argument as to why this framework was wrong.

The most startling thing about this revised version of the report, though, was that the new rationale for the conclusion appeared to be based on only one study – at least, only one was cited for it. The task force had said they really wanted to look at only U.S. studies since those in other countries would have a different context, but this study used British women who have a screening requirement the U.S. doesn't have. There are several other problems with this study.[1]

Yet the fact of many flaws isn't really the point, since in the real world all studies have some flaws. Far more important is that the study doesn't support the conclusion, since it did find more drug overdoses in women who had abortions compared to others.[2] Also important is that it doesn't even address the conclusion. It was only looking at extreme outcomes – drug overdoses rather than over-all substance abuse, for example.

There is a clear rule on what to do with one study, and here it is:

> Do not interpret a single study's results as having importance independent of the effects reported elsewhere in the relevant literature. The thinking presented in a single study may turn the movement of the literature, but the results in a single study are important primarily as one contribution to a mosaic of study effects.[3]

This comes from another APA Task Force, so it's official. We don't draw such a sweeping conclusion from only one study. We put together a group of studies so that the flaws may balance out. Setting aside the quality of the study itself, citing only one study in support of a politically-desired conclusion cannot be explained in any other way than a politically-motivated exercise. This is not a debatable point. This is Quantitative Research 101.

So I immediately sent out a memo to the APA governance committees who were now reviewing the report, in case they missed it – it was buried on then page 66. In the actual released report, it's on page 68; look for the conclusion and note the lone one-study citation in parentheses.[4]

There was no response to the memo, nor did a member of the Task Force with whom I had previous friendly conversations reply to an email with this concern.

Consistent Life, upon noting a quarter of Council members had changed with the new year, sent out its letter again. This time it got a response from APA's president, and sent another response.[5] Many other people sent letters as well, making various points. Naturally, this included post-abortion women who were concerned that their voices were being ignored.

Finally came the APA Council meeting of August 13, 2008, which was to vote on whether or not to accept and disseminate the Report. Because the story had already broken in the *Wall Street Journal* the previous day, this was the first item on the agenda. It needed to be, because the article had caused the press release announcing the study to be sent out that previous day – as if it had already been approved by the Council.

Speaking for it were endorsers and people commenting that it was good science on the grounds that it was done by good scientists.

I approached the microphone and started to speak as others had, but the president interrupted and said he didn't recognize me as a member of the Council; was I one? I said no. He said I would then need permission to speak. I asked for it, and he gave it so long as I was short. I was told later that it is exceedingly rare that anyone outside of Council is allowed to speak at all.

That may help account for the fact that once I made points similar to the above, no one commented on them. To this moment, I don't have an answer to the basic point of how one study, whether an excellent study or not, could reasonably be seen as supporting a bold and ideologically-desired conclusion.

The problem is that when I was a reviewer, I was sort of in the ingroup, but when I went to the Council, not being on the Council made me a member of the outgroup. I'll admit I didn't even think to mention my credentials beyond the relevant point of being a reviewer, and had to be reminded to give my name, because I was focused on the content. One person did later comment on the letters Council members had received, with a smirk. No content was commented upon. Ingroup-outgroup dynamics were painfully clear.

The vote to receive the report was near unanimous; I believe 6 abstentions. I was startled as I noticed the vote was taken by raising of hands, right in front of everybody. Could the set-up for group conformity have been any more stark?

I was told by three different Council members that I had courage, more courage than they had to go against the group. One of them, when I first asked her if she had read the report, said, "Yes, I read the damned thing." Our lengthy conversation made it clear that she thought it was bad science. But she didn't raise this objection at the meeting.

Of all the people who ought to know better than to pressure for such group conformity, those who study psychology should have seen red flashing alarm bells going off at this. Many disasters have been caused when people submit so strongly to the thinking of the group that they're afraid to rock the boat; Irving Janis started the idea of "groupthink" with this, showing how it worked with Kennedy administration's Bay of Pigs fiasco.[6]

WHAT CAN WE CONCLUDE?

The APA Task Force Report dismisses many of the studies of post-abortion trauma on the grounds that women were already traumatized by the time they showed up to the abortion clinic. This is surely true, but doesn't it then follow that it's highly irresponsible to simply give them surgery and then send them home? If we have clear and undisputed information that a disproportionate amount of women traumatized by such things as domestic abuse or already suffering from substance abuse or depression are showing up at any medical location, how can it be reasonable medical care to not screen for this and provide opportunity for intervention? I pointed this out in my review, but they didn't see this point as worthy of inclusion.

Meanwhile, the Report and the press release about it do say that there are groups that have higher negative aftermath, including teenagers, women who are pressured or ambivalent, women who have more than one, and those with late-term abortions. This is information we can put forth as at least being a consensus among all researchers.

The 91-page Report is definitely worth reading for people who wish to be familiar with this area, because it's true that there are a lot of complications that come with trying to study this. There tends to be a high drop-out rate of post-abortion women in doing studies long-term, and of course long-term is needed to know what's really happening. Women who've had abortions often won't admit to it in surveys, so they'd slip in with the group who actually haven't, making it impossible to really compare those who have to those who haven't. Large medical databases will let the researcher know who did have abortions, but then we also need to take into account all kinds of other traumatizing events that go along with the abortions. To be rigorous in making a scientific case, researchers will need to know all the alternative explanations and arguments from the view that is sure it's not abortion itself that is inherently traumatizing; in short, to add the balance of views that the task force never had by including its view among others.

But as for the Report's conclusion of no evidence of negative aftermath for adult women with an unplanned pregnancy who do choose one first-trimester abortion, we know this much: if it were clearly supported by the evidence, then they would have been able to find it out still following their own rules. They clearly wanted very badly to convince people of that conclusion. If they couldn't do it while still following the rules of science, then there can be no other reason than that it couldn't be done.

In a 1976 case before the United States Supreme Court, not long after *Roe v. Wade*, Justice White observed, "I am not yet prepared to accept the notion that normal rules of law, procedure, and constitutional adjudication suddenly become irrelevant solely because a case touches on the subject of abortion."[7] Unfortunately, there are many other people who are so prepared.

CHAPTER TEN
THE POLITICAL MOVEMENT

PALTRY SUPPORT

People in the pro-choice movement provide the theory that underpins the whole operation. Supportive services of lobbying for the needed laws and working with the media are provided. Attempts for increasing public acceptance are constant. With all that, it would seem that a social movement dedicated to keeping abortion available would be among the first places to go to get emotional support services for abortion staff when that becomes necessary.

Dr. Hern, in one of his *New York Times* editorials, complains.

> Prochoice organizations often ignore, patronize and disparage the contributions of physicians who specialize in abortions, in contrast with their support for well-known physicians in conventional specialties who perform some abortions.[1]

In the 1993 Project Choice survey, abortion doctors were asked if they felt that pro-choice organizations and politicians were doing enough to support those who provide abortion care. Over 78 percent responded no. That means that almost four-fifths of the 961 abortion doctors who answered feel that they don't get enough support from the social movement they would most reasonably expect it from.

Here are some pertinent comments from the survey:

#48: The pro-choice majority has done nothing to support physicians that provide abortion service. It seems that even pro-choice women are reluctant to go to an office that provides abortion care, for fear that they may be thought to be obtaining an abortion.

#97: I feel many of the local pro-choice organizations and their members are more interested in discussing the issues at a wine and cheese party than getting out on the front lines.

I have heard women state they go to Dr. "X" because they are pro-choice. These various Dr. X's frequently talk a good game and have busy practices, but I have yet to see them provide abortions. Privately they tell me they are afraid to lose patients and physician referrals. I wish I had the luxury of reaping the rewards of being pro-choice without the above problems.

#212: The "GOOD OL' GIRL" network refers around me because I operate a surgical service not a socio-political one.

Pro-life picketers are in constant touch with counter-picketers, and so the attitudes of their most rambunctious opponents are constantly available to them. They report that it's quite common that the people who are putting so much of their time and effort into defending the clinics actually have contempt for the doctors themselves. Remarks about them being in it for the money are not uncommon.

A more official example of this kind of attitude was given by Marge Brerer, in a workshop entitled "Feminist Perspectives and Reactions" at a conference on RU-486. The following remarks were taken from an audiotape of the conference.

> Abortion providers, if they are to offer women an open choice between this new method, and vacuum aspiration – and I don't think it's at all clear that abortion providers as a group, let alone as individuals, are going to be willing to give women an open choice – in fact, I think there's some indication that the opposite may be the case – then they will need to explain the differences and similarities in a coherent and accurate way to women.

Women have often said that they see the provider as having a supportive role. I would like to ask whether providers will still be able to have a punitive role, if that's the role they want to have.[2]

More recently, an article in the journal *Sociology of Health and Illness* outlined several ways in which physicians and activists have "an uneasy alliance."[3]

HALTING VIOLENCE?

All that work put in on influencing public opinion doesn't necessarily help, either. The most clear-cut, definitive example of this is what occurred when one man, who had been picketing for only a short time and had not attended meetings, went behind an abortion clinic without the knowledge of any of the picketers and shot Dr. David Gunn point blank, and then turned himself in.

At this point, the pro-choice movement and the media swung in to action. Did they take the sensible actions necessary to try to prevent this from happening again? Did they strain to avoid any copy-cat stunts? No, they swung in to action to gain full PR advantage in showing how awful the right-to-life movement is. They used it for propaganda purposes, and that was more important than preventing its recurrence.

Nor did they find it nearly as newsworthy when a woman died June 26, 1994 of hemorrhaging caused by an abortion at that same location, Pensacola Women's Medical Services. The *Pensacola News Journal* did a front page story on June 29, 1994. Local coverage of such deaths is common, but national coverage is rare.

The prudent thing to do after an appalling event of that kind is to show the outrage of the entire community, including, and especially, prolifers. After all, there are nuts who would be willing to take condemnation, as long as they're regarded as heroes by the people with whom they identify. If they are denounced by fellow abortion opponents, then the chance of another crime to fit the pattern is lowered considerably. There may be some individuals with the philosophy and the fortitude to put up with universal rebuke, but the anger of the pro-life movement against those who commit violent acts is the best defense the abortion staff has.

The pro-life movement immediately jumped in to give that very assurance. All major and almost all minor pro-life groups sent out press releases at once, and made spokespersons available. Preventing violence by making it absolutely clear that they couldn't stand it was something all the leadership was eager to do. The media and the pro-choice movement had the tools necessary to take that rational approach. But they decided that showing off the prolifers to be nasty people was more important.

They hunted up fringe people to defend the slaying. All movements have nuts, and they can be found if they are searched for. Every movement that has ever existed has had its "lunatic fringe." The pro-choice movement is no exception. If ever anyone in the media takes a notion to apply the same standards to that movement as are applied to prolifers, they will find plenty of material, from minor acts like throwing urine and feces on demonstrators to major acts like trying to run them down with their cars. Prolifers carried away by ambulances due to attacks from counter-demonstrators is not regarded as newsworthy.

Prolifers don't usually make a big deal of the violence aimed at them. The media have made it clear that they don't care. From the prolifers' point of view, once babies are being torn limb from limb, bringing up the fact that someone put out a lit cigarette on your bare skin seems kind of petty. A large portion of prolifers hold a "turn the other cheek" philosophy, and they know that the pro-choice movement as a whole is not responsible for its lunatic fringe. Most pro-choice people would never think to engage in such violence, and it would be unfair to paint the movement with a broad brush based on the actions of a few of its members.

To do the logical thing for preventing violence against abortion staff at that point would have obligated the media to show prolifers as actually being reasonable people. Showing them as irrational was more important than protecting the abortion industry from violence. The pro-choice movement spent a great deal of time and energy in a strategy that was blatantly counter-productive as far as protecting abortion staffers is concerned.

The most clear-cut illustration of this is the way the television news show "Nightline" treated the first shooting incident. They originally scheduled Nancy Myers, spokesperson for the National Right to Life Committee, the largest pro-life group. She would have condemned the shooting in no uncertain terms. They cancelled her. Who did they bring on in her place? Paul Hill – the man responsible for the second shooting incident.

The media gave Hill so much press coverage that they built up his delusions of grandeur. Though prolifers were appalled and did what they could to counter his fringe vigilante views, the media could not have done a more efficient job of guaranteeing another incident if that had been their plan.

There were at least eight doctors that quit performing abortions after the first shooting. The reason given was fear, and a sense that terrorism was being practiced. The media and pro-choice movement, when mentioning this at all, used it as another propaganda advantage. It never seemed to occur to them that part of the anxiety these doctors might be unconsciously feeling was the knowledge that the very people that were being counted on for support were in fact more interested in putting prolifers down than in actually protecting the doctors.

COGNITIVE DISSONANCE AGAIN

When *60 Minutes* ran a piece about Hillview abortion clinic in Maryland, showing the women who had been killed and maimed, they made the suggestion that perhaps greater regulation was necessary. To this the head of the National Abortion Federation, Barbara Radford, said, "We want to make sure that women have choices when it comes to abortion services. And if you regulate it too strictly, you then deny women the access to service."

Not many women want access to unqualified anesthesia services that leave them paralyzed.

On that same report, when pro-choice Maryland state senator Mary Boergers wanted legislation to regulate clinics because of this scandal, she lost pro-choice support. When she acted for all the world as if she believed that "safe and legal" really meant *safe*, she was called on the carpet. She said that if you ask questions, "They then treat you as if you're the enemy."

An insistence on not asking questions should be a major contradiction to the minds of many who believe in the pro-choice philosophy. In fact, it is also a mark of dealing cognitive dissonance, with a contradiction in ideas.

Luhra Tivis was disturbed at events at Dr. Tiller's clinic. "When I went to the leaders in NOW in Wichita, and told them what was going on, they said, we agree with you, but we can't rock the boat." She says that a woman from the local chapter of NOW wrote a piece for the newsletter criticizing Tiller, but they pulled it. They said they weren't going to rock the boat. NOW is not normally known for being reticent about rocking the boat where women's welfare is concerned.

Since a large portion of the pro-choice movement lays claim to being motivated by feminism, the contradictions with other parts of feminism provide a big source of strain caused by cognitive dissonance.

An example would be the attitudes on women's bodies. This story comes from *The New Our Bodies, Ourselves*: "When I found out I was pregnant, I was frightened and angry that my body was out of my control. I was furious that my IUD had failed me, and I felt my sexual parts were alien and my enemy."[4] Other parts of the book insist that we accept our bodies and reject notions of biological inferiority. Women being in touch with our bodies and viewing them positively is an important principle of the book, which they here contradict without blushing.

Another example is when on National Public Radio the chair of the National Women's Political Caucus (NWPC), Harriet Woods, was asked if pro-life women were welcome in the organization. She responded, "Only if they kept their beliefs about abortion in the dark." Yet one of the co-founders of the NWPC, Fannie Lou Hamer, said that she believed that legal abortion was legal murder.[5] Ms. Woods was proposing to silence one of the founders of the group. She was only *proposing* it, of course. If Fannie Lou Hamer had still been alive, there wouldn't have been any way that anyone would have succeeded in silencing her. She made too many sacrifices for the civil rights movement and other anti-violence movements for human dignity, and she was not the reticent type. But the fact that Harriet Woods could, with a straight face, suggest that a woman's right to abortion was more important that a woman's right to speak her mind shows some internal inconsistency in her thinking.

Nevertheless, there are some well-known feminists who favor abortion availability who have noticed that there are some problems with the consistency between feminism and abortion. For example, Germain Greer in an interview in *The New Republic* commented,

> It is typical of the contradictions that break women's hearts that when they avail themselves of their fragile right to abortion they often, even usually, went with grief and humiliation to carry out a painful duty that was presented to them as a privilege. Abortion is the latest in a long line of non-choices that begin at the very beginning with the time and the place and the manner of lovemaking.[6]

Naomi Wolf caused quite a stir in an article she wrote for a later issue of *The New Republic* with remarks like,

> How can we charge that it is vile and repulsive for pro-lifers to brandish vile and repulsive images if the images are real? To insist that the truth is in poor taste is the very height of hypocrisy. Besides, if these images *are* often the facts of the matter, and if we then claim that it is offensive for pro-choice women to be confronted by them, then we are making the judgment that women are too inherently weak to face a truth about which they have to make a grave decision. This view of women is unworthy of feminism."[7]

Feminists also have a problem that can be illustrated by the man who, passing by a pro-life literature table, announced, "If my girlfriend is stupid enough to get pregnant, she's going to the abortion clinic that afternoon, whether she wants to or not." This position is clearly antichoice, but pro-abortion. Cases of this kind of attitude are so common that there's no way that anyone active on either side of the issue can have failed to run across it. Letting the ramification of it sink in is another matter.

On a different approach, it was a common argument that having abortion readily available would help to solve several social problems. There would be fewer births out of wedlock and children with single mothers or on welfare. Teen suicides resulting from unwanted pregnancies would go down, and the crime rate would also go down as the frustrations of being an unwanted child would disappear. Abortion would see to it that no unwanted children remained.

The actual results? In 1960, 5.3 percent of births were outside of marriage. In 1970, with abortion available in more states, that was up to 10.7 percent. In 1990, it was at 26.2 percent. Children with single mothers were eight percent in 1960, 22 percent in 1990. The children on welfare have gone from 3.5 percent to 11.9 percent in that time. The teen suicide rate went from 3.6 percent to 11.3 percent, and reported violent crime has gone from 16.1 per 100,000 to 73.2.

Child abuse rates have skyrocketed. The U.S. National Center of Child Abuse and Neglect reports around 167,000 cases in 1973, and by 1991 it soared to around 2.5 million cases. This is consistent with an alternative idea of what millions of abortions might do: that abortion might act as other violence does, by serving as a model, and by desensitizing.

Correlation is not causation. Just because all these things have skyrocketed at the same time abortion did does not mean that abortion caused them. But those who would wish to make the argument that there is a connection would have these facts to back them up, and those that argue the opposite don't.

Does that keep abortion proponents from continuing to use these arguments? Of course not. It's supposed to have that beneficial effect, and that's all there is to it.

The argument as to why current abortion practice might by a contributing factor to the rise in crime is best explained by former United States Surgeon General Joycelyn Elders. "Our children are dying because they are being taught to use violence to solve problems. Violent behavior is being modeled in our homes, schools, neighborhoods, and in the media. Children are learning daily that violence is a socially acceptable response to others' behavior."[8]

Gloria Steinem also caught this point, as shown in her book *Revolution from Within*. "We have come to realize that the devaluing of animal life is a kind of training ground for devaluing all life." This negatively impacts our society, "because the truth is we cannot harden our hearts selectively."

Both of these women see no contradiction in what they say and in their staunch support of abortion. Unless they say that abortion is an exception to the points they're making, we'll presume that's because they hold abortion not to be violence at all. That children will look at a picture of a fetus and announce it to be a baby doesn't mean that those children perceive it as violence to do the fetus in. Animal life is different from fetal life.

There is a simple method to find out if this is simply a philosophical difference, or if people who say such things have a strain in the mind caused by the contradiction between these statements and support for abortion. Just ask them if they see a contradiction. If they look puzzled and say no, then perhaps it's a difference of viewpoint. If they bite your head off, there's probably some tension.

CLINIC "DEFENSE"

There are plenty of movements that have activists that are counter-productive, including both sides in the abortion debate. In the case of the pro-choice movement, many of the self-styled "clinic defenders" are brought in by the clinic, but it's also not uncommon for clinics to want them to go away. They aren't always willing to go away. They're more interested in their own philosophies and they don't take orders from the clinic.

The following comes from the Bay Area Committee Against Operation "Rescue" (BACAOR) Manual for Clinic Defense. It illustrates this point, along with belligerency, a little screening out, and some remarkably interesting logic.

We do not call police ourselves during a hit. Our best work is done before police arrive, or when there are not enough police there to prevent us from doing what we have to do. Get in place before cops can mess with it; establish balance of power early, do key acts requiring physical contact with OR as much as possible before cops have enough people to intervene. Even if the sidewalk is "public," we've had success at putting enough of us out, early enough, to basically bully the ORs into staying across the street.

Another section says: "Even if the scuffle gets to a heated point, they are going to stop eventually, either from fear, demoralization or from realization that they are blowing the image they have tried to convey to media and others." The idea that prolifers really mean it when they say they are using nonviolence as with Mohandas Gandhi and Martin Luther King Jr., of course, is not an option.

The term "OR" is short for a protester working with Operation Rescue. The manual goes on to talk about psychological tactics, including that,

while male loose cannons are more capable of hurting defenders than are female loose cannons, it is also true that the men have such a disdain/disregard for women that they are less likely to physically beat people up.

Read this sentence over again: men failing to beat people up follows naturally from having disdain and disregard for women.

Chivalry is not dead with these people (just convoluted), and that means they have an inordinate sense of modesty and 'honor' about being accused of touching women. There are innumerable instances of clinic defenders neutralizing male ORs by shouting 'get your hands off me, don't you dare touch me' all the while they are tugging or pushing OR out of the line.

It doesn't take an abortion opponent to point out that these attitudes aren't helpful in defending the clinics. Clinic personnel have been known to be of that opinion as well. Not all support is supportive.

CHAPTER ELEVEN
COLLEAGUES AND CLIENTS

SUPPORTING ABORTION, NOT ABORTION PROVIDERS

Colleagues in the medical community would seem like a logical place for abortion doctors to go for group support. The old attitudes against abortionists during the illegal period, after all, were against doctors who were willing to do something illegal. Nowadays, the major medical societies, including the American Medical Association and the American College of Obstetricians and Gynecologists, are firmly in the abortion assembly. They use their lobbying influence and professional credentials to support abortion on demand.

Their enthusiasm for abortion availability, however, isn't matched by enthusiasm for those actually doing them.

The Project Choice survey of abortion doctors asked several questions on this point. Almost 70 percent didn't feel that abortion providers are respected in the medical community, and about 65 percent have felt ostracized. Sixty-one percent had been verbally confronted by an anti-abortion physician, and almost 60 percent perceived their prestige as a physician had been damaged by being identified as an abortion provider. Half felt isolated from the rest of the medical community. A shockingly high portion, 19 percent, said they had been denied hospital privilege because of providing abortions.

Carol Joffe, in her admiring book on the lives of several dozen abortion doctors, says "mainstream medicine has long distanced itself from abortion. I will suggest . . . that it is the medical community itself, and not Operation Rescue, that bears chief responsibility for the present marginalization of abortion provision."[1]

Delese Wear interviewed seven abortion doctors in Ohio and found a mixture of views as to whether fellow physicians were supportive. Yet one person did say:

> "I don't get to talk shop with my peers . . . no intelligent conversations with real smart colleagues the way most doctors get to . . . I don't feel like I'm part of the medical community. I'm on my own, floating on an iceberg. I miss feeling connected."[2]

and another summarized the case:

> "Who would want my life? Very few would be willing to put up with the bullshit I do. It's low prestige, medically isolated . . . I have no doctor friends and have very little support from the medical community."[3]

GRATITUDE?

If other doctors and the pro-choice movement are inadequate as sources of support, then surely at least the clients can be expected to be grateful. And of course many of them are. Yet many seriously do not want to be there. This isn't unusual in medicine, but most medicine has on-going care so that the doctor is able to monitor the patient and see that she's improving, allowing for both a sense of accomplishment and gratitude.

The assembly-line set-up of the average abortion clinic is not asking for respect from the clients. In fact, this technique may be employed partly because of knowledge that the gratitude is never really going to come. It's deliberately not asked for.

In a telephone conversation, the Dallas clinic administrator comments on this.

> There's two ways to look at how change happens. One is, we have to get people out there to respect them. But, from my experience, that never works.

For most people they're looking for something bigger than themselves. In abortion, I think this all fits together with how women experience abortion. For many women nowadays, they're angry that they had a choice. It's too bizarre, but it's like, if you weren't here, I wouldn't have had to make this choice. . .

We're working real hard at this clinic to assist women in moving from a place of experiencing themselves as victim of their decision, or of their boyfriend, to moving to a place where they see this differently. I think that the same thing needs to happen with the physician. If the physician is a victim of the anti-abortion movement, or a victim of the other anti-abortion doctors or a victim of Operation Rescue -- no change is going to come from that. Plus, victims are too annoying, you know. They don't invite your participation.

This clinic administrator knows that the lack of appreciation is not only an intense problem, but she's giving up on the idea of fixing it by getting more appreciation. The doctors need inner strength instead.

An abortion doctor who had a problem with inner strength commented on this in the *Boston Globe*. "I could have put up with some more, but I felt no community support at all. I could have taken a lot more abuse, but there was not even a patient saying, 'I know you're not a murderer.' That demoralized me."[3]

THE FEELING IS MUTUAL

Feeling highly stressed can be expected to lead to a lashing out. The lambaste can be aimed at several targets, and for the abortion doctor, there are plenty available. Pro-life picketers are among the best to aim for, but they're outside the building. Throwing barbs at them on the way in and on the way out only does so much. Politicians, media, other doctors, and the pro-choice movement can be complained about, but they're off somewhere else and so can be targeted only verbally. Staff people are close by and can make excellent targets, but they're hired and not likely to stay if they are the butt of too much resentment. Besides, they're in the same fix.

There is one target left that falls into place nicely – the person that the doctor has never seen before and likely will never see again. The person who is going to allow the doctor to come close to her with sharp instruments. The person who makes this whole job necessary, then isn't even grateful.

The doctor can blame the person who, if she had only kept her pants on, wouldn't be doing this. Never mind that there is, in each and every case, another person who could also have prevented it by keeping his pants on. He's not there to lash out at, and she is. Besides, blaming the woman for getting pregnant is traditional.

Current abortion opponents are not the only ones to have noticed this phenomenon. Marjorie Brerer's position is unambiguously in favor of ready access to abortion. Yet on a panel discussion at a conference on RU-486 she listed one of the reasons for someone being an abortion provider as, "a relatively sadistic way of punishing women." She later says that, with RU-486, she, "would like to ask whether providers will still be able to have a punitive role, if that's the role they want to have."[5]

Those that have looked at this in scholarly fashion have found indications of this. "Many faculty and resident physicians doing abortion work reported clinical symptomology. Among these symptoms, the researchers discovered obsession over abortion per se and over the morality of abortion, depression, a need to find 'reasons' for performing the abortions, and anger directed primarily at the aborting women."[6]

Dr. Hern notes: "One respondent expressed increasing resentment of the casual attitudes of some patients considering the emotional cost to those providing the service."[7]

The *American Medical News* article, "Abortion Providers Share Inner Conflicts," indicates that anger at the woman is regarded as a commonplace, especially for women who wait for late terms. "A New Mexico physician said he was sometimes surprised by the anger a late-term abortion can arouse in him. On the one hand, the physician said, he is angry at the woman. 'But paradoxically,' he added, 'I have angry feelings at myself.'"[8] Why is this paradoxical, when he is just as much a participant as she is? Because it's unusual to admit that responsibility lies on everyone involved, and blaming the woman alone is more common.

Another example is recounted in Don Sloan's book, *Abortion: A Doctor's Perspective, a Woman's Dilemma.* Dr. Sloan was an abortionist (his own self-description) who was still in the field and still advocated for it strongly. He tells this story as told to him by one of his patients:

> "I was working upstate, and I got involved with this guy – it was dumb, but I got pregnant. I mean, we both knew it was just a summer thing, that we weren't going to see each other again. Well, I asked around and got the name of a doctor there who did abortions in his office. It wasn't that expensive, a few hundred bucks, and we could get that together between us. I mean, the guy was all right, he just wasn't the love of my life. So I made an appointment.
>
> "The people in the office seemed real nice, so I was kind of surprised by this guy. He kind of leered at me, you know? But at the same time he really had an attitude – like I was dirt or something. I thought, was it 'cause I'm black? But I think it was just him.
>
> "He said, 'Get your things off and lie down.' And I'm thinking isn't there a gown or something? I was standing right there. So I asked for some place to change and he said, 'Do it here. We have to get this over with.' But he gave a sheet to wrap up in, which was clean, at least.
>
> "When I went to put my feet in the stirrups, my legs were too long. And while he's adjusting them, he's making these cute little remarks about my legs and my nail polish. I'd already paid, and I wanted to get it over with too, or I'd have been out of there, I swear. I was that angry.
>
> "It hurt – a lot. And I could hear the suction thing – it was real loud, and it was like it was sucking out my whole insides. I kept asking questions, and the whole time, he didn't say one thing. Just ignored me.
>
> It seemed like an eternity, Keisha said, but it was probably only a few minutes until the doctor told her he was done.
>
> "When I got up, I felt sort of faint, and there was blood running down my leg. I showed him, and he said it was

nothing. But when I went to get my clothes, the blood was getting on the floor. And he said to me, 'You're dirtying things up. Get back up here.' He did some more stuff, and I heard the machine again. It didn't hurt as much, though, or maybe I was just so out of it I didn't care."

He gestured to her to get up again, and this time he gave her a sanitary napkin. 'You know how to use these things, I suppose?' he sneered.[9]

Dr. Sloan blames this unknown doctor's attitude on sexism, a reasonable assessment. He then goes on to relate it to other kinds of sexism in the health care system, as with obstetrics, and he's right that those are areas in need of improvement. Of course, in any individual case, the doctor may have had a major argument with somebody that day and been in a sour mood. Nor would it be fair to draw any conclusions from one incident.

Still, it does fit the pattern. It could be that the doctor was frustrated for the reasons we're talking about now, or it could be that the patient was seeing the symptom of estrangement from others that is a symptom of post-traumatic stress.

Sexism is something that can be gotten rid of, to a large extent, if it's worked on. It certainly can be removed from areas like obstetrics, diagnostic D & C's, hysterectomies, and c-sections. Much progress has been made already, and hopefully more will be made. If that's the problem with abortion, progress will be made there as well. But if the problem is the lashing out or the alienation that goes with PTSD, then progress toward sensitivity to the clients could be harder to come by.

DO WE NEED TO HAVE ONLY DOCTORS DOING ABORTIONS?

One of the few restrictions on abortion that was still allowed by *Roe v. Wade* in 1973 was that the state could require only licensed physicians to do them. This was hailed as a major advance over the back-alley butcher period. Yet now there are people seriously suggesting that one way to ease the shortage of abortion doctors is to allow people with less medical training than doctors to do them.

Abortion providers themselves, however, tend to oppose this suggestion. According to the Project Choice survey, although almost 80 percent perceive that there is in fact a shortage, almost 79 percent do not feel that non-physicians should be allowed to do abortions. About 76 percent of those who said that there is in fact a shortage nevertheless said that the field should not be opened up to people who are not physicians.

Since early abortions are less complicated, it would seem logical that a higher percentage of "early-term" providers would approve of non-physicians being allowed to do abortions than "late-term" providers. But those who only perform first trimesters opposed allowing non-physicians to perform them by almost 84 percent. They opposed it by a higher margin than the respondents as a whole.

Those proposing this haven't looked at the reasons that the pool of practitioners is dwindling so much. They aren't even thinking of addressing the root causes. The dynamics of abortion with medically-trained non-doctors is not going to be that much different from the current situation. The stress is exactly the same, and lack of appreciation isn't likely to be better. The stigma may well be worse. They don't have the aura of prestige a physician would normally get just for being an M.D.

But one of the biggest flaws in this proposal is the assumption that if we add more people to the pool of those legally qualified to do abortions, we will in fact have more people willing to do them. Are all the doctors doing them now going to stay in the field? Are they going to stay when, after all the guff they've had to put up with, they're being told that the work they do can just as well be done by people with less medical training?

The nurse practitioners that are being proposed as alternative abortion providers are primarily women, while current abortion providers are primarily men. The idea that work that men are becoming unwilling to do should be sloughed off on women is causing discomfort to many. But the question of whether this is workable also needs to be asked.

Part of the theory of letting nurse practitioners do abortion is that, as women, they will be more inclined to identify with the woman and give her more tender care. Enough women have had abortions that large numbers of them are in the medical field. Still, the fact remains that women doctors who are already professionally qualified to do abortions are not joining the field in droves. They are under-represented among abortion providers now, and always have been. As of the year 2006, 43.7% of U.S. ob/gyn doctors are female, according to figures from the American College of Obstetricians and Gynecologists. No one has figures for what percentage of abortion doctors are female, but various samplings show that the portion is by far less than that.

Two such women, Suzanne Poppema and Susan Wicklund, who had abortions and went on to high work loads of doing abortions, wrote autobiographical books that show a great deal of empathy toward their women patients. Yet they thereby help show reasons why women may not be attracted to the field. As Dr. Poppema puts it,

> Sorrow, quite apart from the sense of shame, is exhibited in some way by virtually every woman for whom I've performed an abortion, and that's 20,000 as of 1995. The sorrow is revealed by the fact that most women cry at some point during the experience . . . The grieving process may last from several days to several years . . . Grief is sometimes delayed . . . the grief may lie sublimated and dormant for years.[10]

She proceeds to discount post-trauma reactions in women as an "antichoice" ploy. Later, however, she indicates her knowledge of how the dynamic of sexist injustice works in repeat abortions:

> There are psychological factors that come into play regarding repeated unwanted pregnancies. Maybe some women process a traumatic event improperly and unwittingly keep falling into the same behavioral situation. Possibly the birth-control failure has to do with the fact that there's been a very unequal power relationship between the woman and her sexual partner. But in individual cases where women

come to us with repeated need for abortion, I don't speculate as to why.[11]

She's seeing herself as being non-judgmental, but there are other professional women who might get an uncomfortable sense of not wishing to participate in male domination of women; when surgery is required, that amounts to participating in abuse. It would feel more like being an enabler in self-destructive behavior. This may help account for their being relatively discouraged about getting into the field.

Dr. Poppema also relates that when she was employed by a clinic (rather than running her own) and asserted practices that the patients needed, she was actually fired. Such money-making bureaucracy will never sit well with women who have empathy with other women.

As for nurses, the academic literature has already identified the problem that nurses are more likely to be upset by abortion work than doctors are. Nurses are closer to the fetus and more inclined to identify with it, but this has been said by researchers who were clearly favoring abortion availability themselves. The idea wouldn't occur to them that maybe the nurses, being women, were more inclined to identify with the pregnant woman, and thus identify with her in a way that shared her sense of disturbance over going through a traumatic event. Nurse Sallie Tisdale comments, "I watch a woman's swollen abdomen sink to softness in a few stuttering moments and my own belly flip-flops with sorrow."[12] The article in the *American Medical News* gives another example:

> A nurse who had worked in an abortion clinic for less than a year said her most troubling moments came not in the procedure room but afterwards. Many times, she said, women who had just had abortions would lie in the recovery room and cry, "I've just killed my baby. I've just killed my baby. "I don't know what to say to these women," the nurse told the group. "Part of me thinks, 'Maybe they're right'." Such self-doubt is not uncommon to the abortion field.[13]

In both these cases, it is not identifying with the fetus, but identifying with the woman that causes these abortion workers distress.

Allowing non-doctors in may postpone the inevitable by making more providers available, but doesn't address the root causes of why people leave the field. Most ironic of all, it may not even succeed in making more providers available, because it will be a move that strongly discourages medical doctors from abortion practice.

CHAPTER TWELVE
GETTING OUT OF THE BUSINESS

Many people who used to be abortion workers are no longer, but most of them are totally uninterested in discussing the matter any more. It's truly remarkable that there are a good portion of such workers who aren't merely out of the business, but taking their stories to the opposition.

This is extraordinary because in order to join the pro-life movement, they must do much more than people who simply change philosophy on almost any other matter. They have to admit to having participated in numerous killings. That would be exceedingly difficult for any self-respecting person to do.

It's also noteworthy that they can actually do so with a fair degree of comfort. In spite of the stereotype of prolifers as intolerant and dogmatic, the fact is that they welcome former abortion workers, listen to them attentively, and give them moral support.

PULLING OFF THE SCREENING DEVICE

If ignoring what's too painful is a well-used strategy to keep going in the business, what happens when that deliberate cloud is removed from the mind? Former abortion doctor David Brewer said that, at one point, "The reality of what was going on was finally beginning to seep in through my calloused brain and heart."[1] If many people have done this, what insight can we gain from them?

Dr. Bernard Nathanson was instrumental in founding the National Association for the Repeal of Abortion Laws (NARAL), and pioneered in setting up a large abortion clinic in New York City. After some time, he wrote a book explaining why he no longer believed this to be sound public policy. After detailing his learning more about fetal development, he says,

> This evolution of my thinking will sound incredible to many. I was generally aware of these biological developments during the years of my abortion crusade. Three things happened. First, I reflected again on the older knowledge in perinatology. Second, new data were reported all the time. Third, and most important, I opened myself up to the data. When one is caught up in revolutionary fervor, one simply does not want to hear the other side and filters out evidence without realizing it. Until 1973 I was sold of bill of goods. No – let me be honest – I was selling a bill of goods. I had been terribly disturbed by the injustice and hypocrisy of the '60s, the disparity between rich and poor, East Side and West Side. I had seen the victims of self-abortion and hack abortionists. After the fever of activity had cooled, I found myself reflecting on the seeds of our revolution.[2]

Carol Everett, who had run Dallas abortion clinics, also wrote a book about her departure. At one point, she says,

> Upon my return to the clinic, I noticed something was different. From my point of view, women had been dancing in through the front door, singing, "I'm pregnant. . . Do my abortion. . ." But when I got back, I saw that all the women coming in the front door were crying. I'd never noticed that before.[3]

She made inquiries as to why things were different, but the other staff noticed nothing amiss. In fact, it was the same as it had always been. She suddenly saw something that she hadn't seen before, even though it had been there all along.

Dr. Beverly McMillan of Mississippi tells her story:

I think my coming out of the abortion situation – I've heard other people talk about their experiences, and it seems to be sort of similar. It doesn't happen all at once.

I would go in and meet my (ahem) well-counseled patient. I would examine her, then I would do the suction D & C procedure under a paracervical block. After it was all over, I would leave my patient on the table, and I would go over to the suction bottle, and I would take the little sindexkingette out. I'd go outside the room to the sink, where I'd open the sindexkingette up, and I personally would pick through it with a forceps, and I would have to identify four extremities and a spine and skull and a placenta. If I didn't find that, I would have to go back in that room and scrape and suction some more, or else my patients would be showing up in 48, 72 hours just like those women in Cook County with an infected incomplete abortion.

And standing at that sink, I guess I just started seeing these bodies for the first time. I don't know what I did before that. I think I just counted. I was cool. Blood didn't make me sick, I could handle all the guts and gore of medicine just fine. But I started seeing this for the first time, and it started bothering me.

I remember one afternoon in particular . . . the manager of the clinic came up to the sink one day while I was getting ready to go through my little procedure. And she said, "Would you let me see – I've never really seen what y'all look at at the sink." And I said sure. And I started showing her – this happened to be about a 12-week abortion, and that was about the farthest along we went. And that day, as I was showing her, I remember very clearly seeing an arm, and seeing the deltoid muscle. It really struck me that day how beautiful that was. And the thought just flashed through my mind – what are you doing? Here was this beautiful piece of human flesh – what are you doing? And that was one of the very last ones that I did.[4]

Former abortion nurse Joan Appleton put it this way:

I can't remember off-hand what the specific problem was, but we wanted to do the abortion by ultrasound, to make

sure that we had indeed gotten . . . the entire pregnancy.
I handled the ultrasound while the doctor performed the
procedure, and I directed him while I was watching the
screen. I saw the baby pull away. I saw the baby open its
mouth.

I had seen 'Silent Scream' a number of times, but it didn't
effect me. To me, it was just more pro-life propaganda. But I
couldn't deny what I saw on the screen. After that procedure,
I was shaking, literally, but managed to pull it together and
continue on with the day.

That was a sudden incident that was etched on her memory, but
she also had a slower, drawn-out questioning process:

I started out in the pro-choice movement believing that
I was helping women, believing that women had the right
to choose, they had a right to life, they had a right to go
on. I felt when I was counselling women, I was preparing
them, I was helping them with a difficult situation so they
could to on with their lives. I told them that they were the
most important person on this earth, that nothing was more
important than them. And once we see you through this
difficult situation, once this is over, you can go about your
life. You now have a freedom. You can go to college.

Guess what, folks? It didn't happen. I had to stop and say,
what's going on? Why isn't this happening? Instead, you're
going back out, you're getting pregnant again, you're getting
diseases. How am I helping you? Those are the questions
that kept gnawing, and gnawing, and gnawing at me.

I finally decided that my questions were too strong. I
didn't like what was going on . . . I didn't like what we were
doing to women. If it was right, why were they suffering?
What have we done? We forget, we created a monster, and
now we don't know what to do with it. We created a monster
so that we could now be pawns to the abortion industry,
those of us women who really still believe in women's rights.
Those of us who still believe, and care, and are pro-woman,
who still believe that we are worth something, we are
intelligent, we aren't doormats, we aren't something to be
used. And we used ourselves. We abused ourselves.

She knew a pro-life picketer named "Debra", and said this about her:

> I firmly believed, I thought she was a little misled, probably by the male religious leaders of the pro-life movement. I thought she was a little misled, but I really believed she cared about women. And so when my questions did get too strong, I couldn't go the Molly Yard and say, Molly, you got a minute? I went to Debra, and I started asking questions.[5]

Going to the opposition is not an uncommon theme in the tales of leaving. Joy Davis gives this account:

> Over a period of time, certain ones [picketers] I got to care a lot about. And when I started to have these mixed up feelings – maybe I don't believe in abortions anymore. This is killing me. I can't sleep. I'm having nightmares. I don't like who I look at in the mirror. The first person I called was the one that cared about me when I did say I believed in abortions. I called the Lackerbys.
> Dr. Tucker had done a lot of things, that I was trying to get the medical board to do something, I was trying to get the D.A.'s office to do something. And nobody was helping me. I had told them, I had given them the actual written proof of what he had done, and they would not do one thing about it. . . So I said, fine – if they don't care, I don't care. I'm going to go to Alaska, I'm going to let him get off the hook, it's over. . . (but) I've got to go home and make sure I give it one last chance, for these people to do something about the things that he's done. So I came home, nobody would do anything, so I called (my sister), and I said, that's it, I'm not going to try any more, I'm coming to Alaska . . . I'll call you when I have my airline tickets . . . I hung up the phone, I sat down in my recliner, I picked the phone up and called Tom and Mary Lackerby and I said, "Would y'all help me do something? Nobody's doing anything." I told them all about the situation, and things just started falling into place after that.

CARING ABOUT WOMEN

One of the interesting developments in those women who were counseling potential abortion clients when they started a questioning period, was the change in how they counseled. Joy Davis reports,

> If the patient ever saw the ultrasound, they could see a baby. It would be sucking its thumb, most of the time, or moving its hands, or whatever, and it was a very cute thing to see, on the ultrasound. And so, as a rule, Dr. Tucker would always tell us to keep that screen turned away from the patient and never let them see it. So I just took it on myself to start showing them the pictures, and most every one I showed the picture got up and walked out, and changed her mind. I did that for a good while. But basically, Dr. Tucker never found out I did that. He started noticing that I was having a lot of people change their mind, and he questioned me, why are they changing their mind? I would tell him I don't know. I would point out, like, see, look at its little lips, look at its little nose, its eyes.

When asked why she did that she replied, "Because I got to the point I didn't want them to go through. I felt like they were going to die, if they went back there to him."

Carol Everett tells of a similar dynamic:

> I also started taking the women into my office, closing the door, and asking "Why are you crying?"
>
> One young woman in particular said, "My parents would kill me if they knew I was pregnant."
>
> "No, they wouldn't kill you," I heard myself say. (Wait a minute! This wasn't the say to sell abortions! I should take the fear, amplify it, get their money, and push them through!) As if from a stranger's throat, my voice continued. "Your parents love you They'll be disappointed, but they'll stand by you. Would you like for me to go home with you to tell your parents?" This was weird! I was actually looking at

the women differently. I wanted to draw close to them and love them. I thought, "if I don't watch out, I'll be the one leaving the clinic . . . Or worse – there won't be any women having abortions if I keep helping them, encouraging them to tell their parents, talk to their husband or boyfriends. If I'm talking people out of abortions, how am I going to make a living? How will I keep my two children in college with their thousand-dollar monthly allowances, new cars, and the rest of it?" It was business as usual around me, but certainly not business *inside* me.[6]

RELIGION

Though religion is absent in the above examples, religion was not actually absent. Carol Everett found in crucial in her thinking, while Bernard Nathanson found it irrelevant. Ms. Everett had been a regular churchgoer who tithed her abortion money (that is, gave one tenth of it to her church), while Dr. Nathanson was an atheist and remained so at the time he wrote *Aborting America*. (That changed later.)

Atheists can take the approach that, since they don't believe in an afterlife, then an abortion takes away *everything* when the baby is gone. There's no soul to stay on. Atheists also believe that the entire world was unplanned, which might shed some new light on the idea of unplanned pregnancy.

Feminist and anti-violence arguments could also make sense to them, and to most religious traditions as well. People who think for themselves rather than simply following religious dogma can find ample reason to fly the coop of the abortion business.

The Hippocratic Oath, which is one that until recently has been taken by all physicians, came from a religious background of pagan gods that very few take seriously any more. It expressly prohibits inducing abortion. The long history of medical ethics is quite capable of opposing abortion without any religious reference at all.

Therefore, no change of religion is necessary in order to psychologically get out of the abortion business. If providing abortions is dangerous to the human psyche, then differing religious viewpoints can still lead to the same conclusion.

CHAPTER THIRTEEN
COLLAPSE

The better part of my early adulthood was spent being an activist against the arms race, raising concerns about the bad health effect of nuclear weapons and their dangers of destruction. Suppose you had come to me in those days and told me the Soviet Union would collapse into its component republics, and the arms race would wind down as tensions decreased because of a popular pro-democracy upsurge in Russia.

I would have told you that I enjoyed the impishness of that idea, but it wouldn't have struck me as realistic. Ideas seemed a little too entrenched to allow for that. But there were underlying weaknesses in the Cold War situation that led to the dynamic which, in hindsight, looks more like it was inevitable. History shows that many things aren't as entrenched as they might appear.

DROPPING SUPPLY

Part of the demand for abortion is being driven by supply. Some women have no thought of getting an abortion, but are pressured into it by parents, partners, or bosses. Some are talked into it by doctors and abortion counselors. A good large number feel ambivalent about the decision. In all those cases, the proximity of the clinic makes a difference.[1] Pressure is likely to be more intense, and be more likely to have an effect, if that clinic is close by. Those that profit from abortion have to be right there in order to talk women into it. Anyone who feels ambivalent about the decision in the first place might find a three-hour trip daunting enough to avoid it. In short, as the number of doctors and clinics decline, abortions will become more limited to those women who actually are determined to get them.

Occasional local news coverage of malpractice suits, lost medical licenses, and scandalous conditions will also add to an image that will leave people less eager.

As supply becomes harder to come by, some couples will be more careful about getting pregnant. They will either avoid sex or be more careful with contraception. If the availability of abortion means people get a little sloppy about remembering to get the diaphragm during a moment of passion, that three-hour trip may help serve as a reminder. A ten-hour trip all the more so.

This idea of pregnancies going down when abortion is less easily available has already been noted in those states that had Medicaid funding of abortion one year, but were suddenly cut off by the Hyde amendment the next year. These could be contrasted with those states that kept the Medicaid funding in spite of the Hyde amendment. The number of abortions went down dramatically, and the number of childbirths went down slightly. The abortions that didn't happen weren't replaced by childbirth. They were replaced by more care about getting pregnant.[2]

Later on, since some states continued to pay for abortions and others did not, a study was done by the Alan Guttmacher Institute, research arm of Planned Parenthood. It found that women in states with Medicaid funding for abortion had an abortion rate 3.9 times higher than women who aren't covered, while in states where Medicaid doesn't fund abortions, Medicaid recipients are only 1.6 times as likely.[3] Poverty causes more abortions than not being in poverty, but having funding available causes more than twice as many yet.

The greater difficulty of getting to an abortion clinic may well spur a greater availability in necessary services to pregnant women. Many maternity homes that had run for decades actually closed down when abortion was legalized, but the current trend is for many more of those to be established again. Schools are having and will have more childcare and educational services available for teenage parents so they can get their degrees and raise their children properly. Workplaces will be more likely to see employees' child-rearing as something to work around, rather than as an intrusion the woman has no right to inflict on them. More women will insist that they should be able to get into the Board of Directors (or to be, say, governor of a state, and still nominated for higher office) without having to leave their babies in the trash outside.

The trend of the recent past in insisting that women must cruelly choose between sacrificing their careers and life plans or instead sacrificing their children will make less and less sense. Women will be in a better position to insist on more rights. Abandoning women to the abortion clinic is a lot harder to do when the abortion clinic is not right there.

DROPPING DEMAND

The number of abortions went up each year from 1973, the year of nation-wide legalization, until about 1981. Then it stayed roughly steady for many years. In the 1990s, it started a significant, steady decline from it peak of around 1.6 million in 1990 to 1.2 million; from 1989 to 2004, a 22% decline.[4]

This decline in numbers is not merely due to lower numbers of women of child-bearing age. The rate is the number of abortions per 1,000 women of child-bearing age, and it has also gone down. According to the Guttmacher Institute, the rate peaked at 29.3 per 1,000 women in 1981, but by 2005 it was 19.4 abortions per 1,000 women between the ages of 15-44.[5] That's about a one-third drop. The ratio of abortions to live births has followed the same pattern.

Here's a crucial part of the trend: over this time, the first-timers of yesteryear became repeaters. By 2002, it had worked up to almost half of those having abortions being their second or more. When there are fewer abortions, but more are repeats, that means that *the number of first-timers has gone down quite dramatically.* It's those that are repeating that are keeping the numbers up as high as they are.

Without those first-timers, from where are the repeaters of tomorrow going to come? Having a first one is a prerequisite to having a second one, so the pool from which the repeaters can come is drying up.

All repeaters will reach menopause eventually. Indeed, since the Guttmacher Institute reports the repeaters tended to be above age 30, for many this is not that far away. Some will become sterile by one means or another before that; some may be inspired to get surgical sterilization if the reported fact is correct that most were using contraception which did not prevent the pregnancy.

Also, quite a few will become prolifers. The most worrisome population trend for the abortion business is that of their own clientele turning into their opposition.

This point is important: the numbers of first-time abortions have gone down far more dramatically than the numbers of abortions as a whole. Women who have a repeat abortion add to the number of abortions but not to the number of women who have had an abortion. As the repeaters drop by attrition, the downturn will become more dramatic.

This can be expected if current trends continue and are not interrupted by governmental pushes to increase them, such as government funding that has so clearly been shown to do so, as documented above.

People have, of course, suggested many ideas on what is causing this downturn. The above discussion about the drop in supply is just one of them.

The Guttmacher Institute, with its connection to Planned Parenthood, suggests better contraception awareness and availability. As would be expected with their philosophy, they don't take into account the possibility that they may have it backwards: in part, people might take more care with contraception as abortion becomes more unworkable.

The timing certainly suggests the impact of various kinds of state laws proposed by the pro-life movement that flooded in with the 1990s. Such laws had been blocked after *Roe v. Wade*, with Justice Blackmun saying informed-consent laws imposed information that wasn't always relevant to the woman's decision. With the *Casey* decision, these were suddenly allowed so long as they didn't impose an "undue burden." Laws such as informed consent or right-to-know have helped with women knowing about fetal development and availability of alternatives. Because of the ability to compare different states, a study by Michael

New provides evidence suggesting that parental-involvement laws have helped cause a substantial drop for minors.[6] The case is strengthened by noting that Maryland had a similar abortion rate to the country as a whole in 1991 and 1992 when it enacted a "Freedom of Choice Act" that swept away any possibility of such laws; the rate went up 8% in the same period (1991-2005) when the national rate went down by 9%.[7]

Evidence also suggests that the greater availability of alternatives, with governmental economic and social supports, have a major impact.[8] This makes sense because women of lower income tend to be more likely to oppose abortion but also more likely to get abortions, meaning both that they are feeling economic pressure to have the abortion but are more easily talked out of it when that pressure is lessened. The fact that crisis pregnancy centers to provide one-on-one help to women have proliferated and now vastly outnumber abortion clinics could also be part of this trend.

Beyond policy, there are other things happening in U.S. society. The "little sister effect" is the term for younger women noticing from their older sisters who had an abortion that it didn't seem to be as much of a problem-solver as they originally thought, and served as a negative role model of something not to do. Another development was the more widespread and easy availability of ultrasound photos, with people showing pre-natal photos with pride as a natural part of their baby-photo collection.

Direct anti-abortion volunteer education efforts of various kinds, covering both the negative experience of abortion for women and the humanity of the unborn child, can also probably be credited. Yet this point is important about those educational efforts: because of the human mind's drive for consistency, those efforts become more effective when the downturn is pointed out. There was a while when there were pro-lifers who were skeptical of the figures and assumed that they needed to assure people that they were still inordinately high in order to move them to action. They had a basic misunderstanding of how the mind works. It's lower numbers that actually move people to action.

THE LAW

Legal changes can sometimes ratify social changes, rather than causing them. The history of Truman Medical Center in Kansas City, Missouri, can provide a good example of how this works.

In the early 1980s, Missouri prolifers were upset that this public hospital was a major abortion center in the city. Having failed to convince its Board of Directors, they went to the Missouri Assembly in the hope of legislation which would cut off a portion of Truman's funding unless they stopped doing abortions. This became a major press story, and the spokespeople for Truman announced that they absolutely would not stop. The public funds were not used for abortions, but for the medical needs of poor patients. If the funds were cut, then the needs of the poverty-stricken patients would not be met. They declared that the prolifers were unfeeling about the needs of the poor. Prolifers countered that it was the Truman staff's stubbornness about performing abortions that would be the cause of the cut-off, but the press as usual took Truman's side and the prolifers withdrew. Legislation was not going to cause a change in this case.

Change, however, was caused. After a time, a new doctor was appointed to head up the ob-gyn department, and his enthusiasm for abortion was considerably less than his predecessor's. He made it fairly clear to the interns and residents that this really wasn't expected of them. Since the interns knew they made no positive impression performing them, and since very few had much enthusiasm to start with, the numbers went down. Poor women were no longer talked into abortions that they hadn't thought of as they had been before, and the bunching up of abortion appointments was stopped.

Earlier, if a woman called up and said that she wanted an abortion, they would make an appointment for her, and that would be the time when about a dozen women would come in. After the change of circumstances, if a woman wanted an abortion, they would tell her to find a doctor to do it, and it could be done there if they wanted to use the facilities. Under that arrangement far fewer were done.

It was at that point the law passed the Missouri legislature which then wound its way through the courts as the *Webster* case. In 1989, when the Supreme Court decided that Missouri could in fact disallow abortions to be done at hospitals that have public funding, the spokespeople at Truman said that was fine. The earlier resistance had evaporated. They had done so few abortions the previous year that it was a small matter to simply cut them out completely.

In this case, the law didn't cause the change. The change happened first, and then the law came and made it thorough and permanent.

Lowering the number of feticides is not merely a worthy goal in and of itself. High numbers are an obstacle to changes in public policy, and low numbers help remove resistance to various kinds of protective legislation or policy changes. Honest and nonviolent methods of lowering abortion numbers therefore not only save lives in the short term, but are the most sound strategy for long-term changes.

THE GREAT SWITCH

The theory of cognitive dissonance plays a great role in all this. In the 1970s and 1980s, the elements were:

(1) The abortion business was expanding. There were more and more clinics, and the numbers were climbing or maintaining themselves at a very high rate, and

(2) We Americans are a noble and virtuous people.

That first one was a fact, and being a fact makes it more resistant to change. It can be unknown, it can be ignored, but it can't be made to be untrue.

The second point, on the other hand, involves our own self-respect. That makes it all the more resistant to change. Many prolifers may have decided that it simply wasn't true, but of course the public in general would be unwilling to.

If both elements resist change, then the tension can best be dealt with by deciding that they don't conflict.

Any attack on the first point will be seen by many as an attack on the truthfulness of the second point. Prolifers have not merely been decrying the morality of abortion. Within their denunciation of abortion is a denunciation of the good will of the American population.

The most daunting obstacle of all for abortion opponents has been that as long as the first point is a fact, then people must either decide that the second point isn't true or that the two points agree with each other. Trying to convince them that the points don't agree with each other leaves them with no other alternative other than to decide the second point isn't true. That point involves the most basic self-respect, and so people are unwilling to do this. Therefore, efforts to persuade them that the two points don't agree runs up against a major brick wall.

There would be the alternative of saying that, because the second element is true, therefore, the first element is not going to last. This point is more easily made when the first element actually starts a process of not lasting.

Under current conditions, (1) Abortion numbers are declining, fewer doctors are willing to do them, and clinics are scarcer, and (2) We Americans are a noble and virtuous people.

In fact, once the first element has changed, it becomes reasonable to suggest that the second element caused the first. At least, the second point, so important to collective self-esteem, is actually strengthened by saying that it caused the change.

In the earlier decades, the dynamics of tension reduction strategies for cognitive dissonance, with the crucial importance of self-respect, were working against the anti-abortion position. But a great switch is under way. Under the new facts, the same dynamic starts working in favor of the anti-abortion position.

Some ruminations taken from a *Newsweek* article called "Virgin Cool" by Michele Ingrassia (October 17, 1994) illustrate how this is working. "Abortion, never an easy alternative for anyone, is even more daunting when you're young. Back in the '70s – and even the '80s – any woman worth her *Ms.* subscription knew she could pass around the hat in her dorm and collect a few hundred bucks for an abortion. Access was rarely a problem: every big city and most college towns had a clinic or at least an abortion doctor, and if he wasn't Marcus Welby, well, at least he had an office . . . . The climate has chilled; even ardent pro-choicers don't treat 'choice' so lightly."

Take special note of the phrase, "and if he wasn't Marcus Welby, well, at least he had an office." As a sense of collapse proceeds, it will be more and more safe to admit things like that. It will be more psychologically safe to bring scandals to public attention.

In fact, it will be needed to help us account for our behavior.

Other possibilities for accounting for our behavior abound. The new information on the possible link of abortion to breast cancer, especially of a first pregnancy among teenagers with a family history of breast cancer, would be one possibility. People will be more open to hearing information on emotional aftermath. The injustice of the situations that push women into abortion is regarded with greater concern when abortion itself is not seen as a minor matter.

After detailing how few abortion doctors there were left, the ABC network news broadcast on January 16, 1998 went to a story on how technology is showing us the fetus more clearly, and showed examples. Then they had a report on Project Rachel, a post-abortion group counseling effort of the Catholic Church. Both the fetal pictures and the positive coverage of a pro-life program were unusual for network news, but are a reasonable response to the information they had just covered on lower availability. If it seems inevitable, the next thing to do is account for why – and figure out how to live with the new situation.

When the behavior is a decline in abortions, our explanations for it will naturally be different than when the behavior is an increase. As more and more people realize that our behavior has changed, and seek to find ways to explain it, we will find more and more examples to illustrate this dynamic.

Most of the public for all these years was highly uncomfortable with abortion. Most supporters weren't enthusiastic, but people were willing to put up with the status quo. When the facts of the status quo change, most people find this a great relief.

Most people have really been wishing that the whole problem would just go away. While we all know that it won't go away completely any time soon (any more than rape or child abuse), the hope that it will becomes less widespread appears slowly but surely to be coming true. The middle position, which is uncomfortable with abortion bans but also uncomfortable with abortion itself, is getting its wish.

The accommodation to abortion never really brought relief of the tension felt, but the collapse of the institution does bring relief. People won't want that relief taken from them.

The "Great Switch" will be powerful, because people want it. They want to avoid despair. They want hope. Once it looks possible, once it looks safe to express the desire that it actually happen, then like the people of the former Soviet Union, it will be a dynamic too powerful to resist.

NOTES

Chapter One

1. Rachel K. Jones, Mia R. S. Zolna, Stanley K. Henshaw and Lawrence B. Finer. "Abortion in the United States: incidence and access to services, 2005, *Perspectives on Sexual and Reproductive Health,* 2008, 40(1):6–16. Text at www. guttmacher.org/pubs/psrh/full/4000608.pdf

2. The report on the Project Choice survey was self-published by its pro-life sponsor, Life Dynamics. It had no peer review and would never pass Institutional Review Board standards due to the use of subterfuge, as can be seen by its name. It therefore does not meet the standards for academic literature, and despite its use of percentages should be regarded as a descriptive and non-scholarly source.

3. Diane M. Gianelli, "Abortion Providers Share Inner Conflicts," *American Medical News*, July 12, 1993.

4. Warren M. Hern and Billie Corrigan, "What About Us? Staff Reactions to the D & E Procedure," Boulder Abortion Clinic. *Advances in Planned Parenthood* 15(1):3-8, 1980

5. Gianelli, see note 3.

Chapter Two

1. Rachel M. MacNair, *Perpetration-Induced Traumatic Stress: The Psychological Consequences of Killing.* (Westport, CT: Praeger, 2002).

2. Marianne Such-Baer, "Professional staff reaction to abortion work," *Social Casework*, July 1974.

3. Kathleen M. Roe, "Private troubles and public issues: Providing abortion amid competing definitions," *Social Science and Medicine* 29 (1989): 1197.

4. Patricia Lunnenborg, *Abortion, A Positive Decision*. (New York: Bergin & Garvey, 1992).

5. Delese Wear, "From Pragmatism to Politics: A Qualitative Study of Abortion Providers" *Women & Health*, Vol. 36(4), 2002, pp. 103-113.

6. Carol E. Joffe, *Doctors of Conscience*. (Boston: Beacon Press, 1995).

7. Don Sloan, M.D. with Paula Hartz, *Abortion: A Doctor's Perspective, A Woman's Dilemma*. (New York: Donald I Fine, Inc., 1992).

8. Suzanne Poppema with Mike Henderson, *Why I Am an Abortion Doctor*. (New York: Prometheus Books, 1996).

9. Susan Wicklund with Alan Kesselheim, *This Common Secret: My Journey as an Abortion Doctor*. (New York: PublicAffairs, 2007).

10. Sallie Tisdale, "We Do Abortions Here," *Harpers*, October 1987

11. Gianelli, see Chapter 1, note 3.

12. Hern and Corrigan, see Chapter 1, note 4

13. *Ibid.*

14. Wicklund, 46

15. Wicklund, 93

16. Howard D. Kibel, M.D., "Editorial: Staff Reactions to Abortion," *Obstetrics and Gynecology*, 39(1), January, 1972.

17. Nancy B. Kaltreider, M.D., Sadja Goldsmith, M.D, M.P.H., and Alan J. Margolis, M.D., "The impact of midtrimester abortion techniques on patients and staff," *American Journal of Obstetrics and Gynecology*, vol. 135, p. 235-238, 1979. quote page 237.

18. Sadja Goldsmith, M.D, M.P.H., Nancy B. Kaltreider, M.D., and Alan J. Margolis, M.D. "Second Trimester Abortion by Dilation and Extraction (D & E) Surgical Techniques and Psychological Reactions," unpublished paper, p. 6.

19. Gianelli, see Chapter 1, note 3.

20. Bruce Jancin, "Emotional Turmoil of Physicians, Staff Held Biggest D & E Problem," *Ob. Gyn. News* Vol. 16 No. 24, December 15-31, 1981.

21. Hern and Corrigan, see Chapter 1, note 4.

22. "Meet the Abortion Providers," Videotape. Conference held by Pro-Life Action League, 1989.

23. Bernard N. Nathanson, M.D., *Aborting America.* (Toronto: Life Cycle Books, 1979)

24. Tisdale, see Chapter 2, note 10.

25. *Ibid.*

26. "Meet the Abortion Providers III: The Promoters," Audiotape. Conference held by the Pro-life Action League, April 3, 1993.

27. *Ibid.*

28. Carol Everett with Jack Shaw, *Blood Money*, (Oregon: Multnomah Press Books, Questar Publishers, Inc., 1992) 21. Names have been removed.

29. Tisdale, see Chapter 2, note 10.

30. Hern and Corrigan, see Chapter 1, note 4.

31. Jancin, see note 20.

32. Such-Baer, 438.

33. *Trauma and the Viet-Nam War Generation: Report of Findings from the National Vietnam Veterans Readjustment Study* (New York: Brunner/Mazel, 1990) 52-53.

34. Such-Baer, 439.

35. Roe, 1192.

36. Roe, 1194.

37. Gianelli, see Chapter 1, note 3.

Chapter Three

1. Mark Twain, *A Pen Warmed-up in Hell: Mark Twain in Protest*, ed. Frederick Anderson (San Francisco: Harper & Rowe, 1972).

2. Hern and Corrigan, see Chapter 1, note 4.

3. Tisdale, see Chapter 2, note 10.

4. Sloan, 239-240.

5. Everett, 98.

6. Magda Denes, *In Necessity and Sorrow: Life and Death in an Abortion Hospital* (New York: Basic Books, 1976), 64.

7. Tisdale, see Chapter 2, note 10

8. Kibel, se Chapter 2, note 16.

9. *Ibid.*

10. "Meet the Abortion Providers." Videotape, 1989.

11. Roe, 1192.

Chapter Four

1. Leon Festinger, Henry W. Riecken, Jr., Stanley Schachter. *When Prophecy Fails* (Minneapolis: University of Minnesota Press, 1956) (condensed)

Chapter Five

1. Nathanson, 99.

2. "Back-Alley Abortions Still Here For the Poorest Among Us," *Ms.*, May/June 1993, p. 89.

3. "Meet the Abortion Providers III: The Promoters," audiotape by the pro-life Action League, held April 3, 1993.

4. Tisdale, see Chapter 2, note 10.

5. Vince M. Rue, Priscilla K. Coleman, J. J. Rue, and David C. Reardon. "Induced abortion and traumatic stress: A preliminary comparison of American and Russian women." *Medical Science Monitor*, 2004 10(10): SR5-16.

6. Thornburgh, 476 U.S. at 762.

7. Tisdale, see Chapter 2, note 10.

8. Gianelli, see Chapter 1, note 3.

9. *Ibid.*

10. "Warns of Negative Psychological Impact of Sonography in Abortion," *ObGyn News*, February 15-28, 1986
11. Warren Hern, *Abortion Practice*, (Philadelphia: Lippincott-Raven, 1984). Our emphasis.

12. Tisdale, see Chapter 2, note 10.

13. Carol Everett, "What I Saw in the Abortion Industry" (Jefferson City, MO: Easton, 1988).

14. Antiprogestin Drugs: Ethical, Legal and Medical Issues, Arlington, Virginia, December 6-7, 1991

14. Everett, see Chapter 2, note 28.

16. *Ibid.*

17. Gianelli, see Chapter 1, note 3.

18. Sloan, 41.

19. "Doctor's Abortion Business Is Lucrative," *San Diego Union*, 12 October 1980, at B-1, col. 1.

20. Letter from Mrs. Mattie Byrd to Ira Reiner (undated).

Chapter Six

1. "Warns of Negative Psychological Impact of Sonography in Abortion," *ObGyn* News, February 15-28, 1986.

2. Gianelli, see Chapter 1, note 3.

3. *Ibid.*

4. Nathanson, see Chapter 2, note 23.

5. John Thomas Noonan, *A Private Choice*, (New York: The Free Press, 1979), 82.

6. Abraham Lincoln, Speech at Cooper Institute, New York, February 27, 1860, in Works v. 5 147. Italics in original.

7. Thornburgh, 476 U.S. at 762.

8. Rue, et al., see Chapter 5, note 5.

9. Brenda Peterson, *New Age Journal*, September/October, 1993.

10. *Ibid.*

11. Ginette Paris, *The Sacrament of Abortion* (Woodstock, CT: Spring Publications, 1992) 25-27.

12. Ginette Paris, *Pagan Meditations* (Woodstock, CT: Spring Publications, 1986)148.

13. Philip G. Zimbardo, *The Cognitive Control of Motivation: The Consequences for Choice & Dissonance* (Scot Foresmen & Co., 1969).

14. Gianelli, see Chapter 1, note 3.

15. Magda Denes, *In Necessity and Sorrow: Life and Death in an Abortion Hospital* (New York: Basic Books, 1976) 64.
16. Sloan, 167.

17. Mary Krane Derr, Rachel MacNair, and Linda Naranjo-Huebl, *ProLife Feminism: Yesterday & Today.* (Philadelphia, PA: Feminism & Nonviolence Studies Association, 2005). See www.xlibris.com/ProLifeFeminism or http://www.fnsa.org/pfyt.html.

18. Sloan, 171.

19. Sloan, 178.

20. Gianelli, see Chapter 1, note 3.

21. Naomi Wolf, "Our Bodies, Our Souls," *The New Republic*, October, 1995.

22. Tisdale, see Chapter 2, note 10.

23. Sloan, 248.

Chapter Seven

1. Nathanson, 193.

2. Patricia G. Miller, *The Worst of Times.* (New York: HarperCollins Publishers, 1993).

3. Miller, 58-59.

4. Miller, 151-152.

5. Miller, 37-38.

6. Miller, 177.

7. Miller, 61-62.

8 Nathanson, 141.

9. In the United States District Court for the District of Kansas (Kansas City Docket), Case No. 84-20019-01.

10. Lenexa, Kansas Police report 81-2643.

11. Everett, see Chapter 2, note 28.

13. Nat Hentoff, «Today's Back-Alley Abortions,» *Village Voice* Vol 36 Iss 26, June 25, 1991 p 20-21; Nat Hentoff, "Covering up Destructive Abortions" *Village Voice* Vol 36, Iss 25, June 18, 1991 p 20-21. Mr. Hentoff does have a

contrary view of abortion, but the magazine did still publish the pieces.

14. *Ms.* Magazine, May/June 1993, p. 89.

15. Sarah Norton, "Tragedy – Social And Domestic," *Woodhull & Claflin's Weekly*, November 19, 1870.

16. *The Revolution* 4(22)346 (December 2, 1869)

17. Derr, MacNair, and Naranjo-Huebl, see Chapter 6, note 17

18. Miller, 147.

19. Sloan, 61-62.

20. Sources: Governmental Population Commission, Demographic Situation in Poland, reports 1993-2002; the Ministry of Health and Social Affairs, reports 1997-2000; Center of Information Systems of Health Care, report of Statistics Researcher Program of Public Statistics 2001-2005.

21. *Demographic Yearbook,* Central Statistical Office, Warsaw, 1995-2001; Center of Information Systems of Health Care, report of Statistics Researcher Program of Public Statistics 2001-2005.

22. Press Group of Police Headquarters, Statistics Materials, Warsaw 2005

23. *Demographic Yearbook.*

24. Statistics Office of the European Communities

Chapter Eight

1. Denes, 227.

2. Plaintiff's First Amended Complaint, Case No. 84-1969, in the Circuit Court of the Ninth Judicial Circuit in and for Orange County, Florida.

3. Florida Department of Professional Regulation Case #89-001853, Miami Herald October 27, 1989.

4. MA #85-10.

5. CA #D-3191

6. New York Medical Board #11593

7. The Indiana Health Profession Bureau Case #89 MLB 0032. Boston Globe, September 2, 1989

8. DPR Case #0098363; Miami Herald, April 29, 1988

9. Florida Department of Professional Regulation case numbers-102532, 73882, 70744, 75174, 80918, 85142, 94175, 94176,95832, 102527, 102528, 102529, 102531, 102598,103134,103466,103467,103468,103469,103751 103752, 103755, 867793, 86772, 32342, 77112, 886774, 95932

10. *The Clarion-Ledger*, Jackson, Mississippi, by Grace Simmons, September 30, 1989.

11. *The Clarion-Ledger*, Jackson, Mississippi, by Beverly Pettigrew Kraft, November 10, 1990.

12. Kentucky Medical Licensing Board case #190, State Medical Board of Ohio, Florida Department of Health and Rehabilitative Services inspection reports, 1989, *The Miami Herald Tropic Magazine* September 17, 1989.

13. Michigan Case #880-46749-FY Michigan Medical board case #82-202 and California Board of Osteopathic Medical Examiners case #90-6 and OAH #N-37351.

14. Affidavit, The State of South Carolina vs. J. F., Case No. 30159. He was indicted, but the case was never pursued due to his death in a car accident, so he was never convicted.

15. *Boston Globe*, September 2, 1989.

16. See, for example, Susan Brownmiller, *Against Our Will: Men, Women and Rape* (New York: Simon & Schuster, 1975).

Chapter Nine

1. See http://wiki.afterabortion.org/indexphp?title=Gilchrist#Weaknesses for discussion of the one study.

2. A.C. Gilchrist, P.C. Hannaford, P. Frank, C.R. Kay. "Termination of pregnancy and psychiatric morbidity," *British Journal of Psychiatry,* 1995;167:243-248, page 247

3. Leland Wilkinson & Task Force on Statistical Inference, APA Board of Scientific Affairs, "Statistical methods in psychology journals: Guidelines and expectations," *American Psychologist,* 1999. page 602. Full article at http://psycnet.apa.org/index.cfm?fa=main.showContent&view=fulltext&format=PDF&id=1999-03403-008

4. Brenda Major, Mark Appelbaum, Linda Beckman, Mary Ann Dutton, Nancy Felipe Russo, and Carolyn West. Report of the Task Force on Mental Health and Abortion, August 13, 2008. Available on the Internet at http://www.apa.org/releases/abortion-report.pdf

5. http://wthrockmorton.com/2008/07/14/anti-violence-group-expresses-concerns-over-apa-abortion-task-force/.

6. Irving L. Janis, *Victims of groupthink: A psychological study of foreign-policy decisions and fiascoes.* (Boston: Houghton Mifflin, 1972).

7. Planned Parenthood of Missouri v. Danforth, 428 U.S. 52,98 (dissent)

Chapter Ten

1. Warren Hern, "Hunted by the Right, Forgotten by the Left," *New York Times*, 13 March 1993.

2. Antiprogestin Drugs: Ethical, Legal and Medical Issues, Arlington, Virginia, December 6-7, 1991

3. Carol E. Joffe, T. A. Weitz, and C. L. Stacey, "Uneasy Allies: Pro-choice Physicians, Feminist Health Activists and the Struggle for Abortion Rights," *Sociology of Health & Illness*. 2004 Sep Vol 26(6) 775-796

4. Boston Women's Health Book Collective, *The New Our Bodies, Ourselves, A Book By and For Women*, (New York: Simon & Schuster, 1984).

5. Derr, MacNair, and Naranjo-Huebl, 202-212.

6. Germaine Greer, interview in *The New Republic*, 5 Oct. 1992.

7. Naomi Wolf, "Our Bodies, Our Souls," *The New Republic*, 15 Oct. 1995.

8. *U.S.A. Today*, 29 Dec. 1993.

Chapter Eleven

1. Joffe, 6

2. Wear, 108

3. Wear, 112

4. *Boston Globe*, November 11,1994

5. Antiprogestin Drugs: Ethical, Legal and Medical Issues, Arlington, Virginia, December 6-7, 1991

6. Such-Baer, 437.

7. Hern and Corrigan, see Chapter 1, note 4.

8. Gianelli, see Chapter 1, note 3.

9. Sloan, 234-235.

10. Poppema, 125-126

11. Poppema, 135

12. Tisdale, see Chapter 2, note 10.

13. Gianelli, see Chapter 1, note 3.

Chapter Twelve

1. Denes, see Chapter 5, note 15.

2. Nathanson.

3. Everett, see Chapter 2, note 28.

4. "Meet the Abortion Providers," Videotape.

5. *Ibid.*

6. Everett, see Chapter 2, note 28.

Chapter Thirteen

1. James D. Shelton, Edward A. Brann and Kenneth F. Schulz, "Abortion Utilization: Does Travel Distance

Matter?," *Family Planning Perspectives*, Vol. 8, No. 6 (Nov.-Dec., 1976), pp. 260-262

2. P.B. Levine, Amy B. Trainor, and D. J. Zimmerman, "The Effect of Medicaid Abortion Funding Restrictions on Abortions, Pregnancies and Births," *Journal of Health Economics,* Vol. 15, 1995, pp. 555-578.

3. Heather Boonstra and Adam Sonfield, "Rights Without Access: Revisiting Public Funding of Abortion for Poor Women," The Guttmacher Report on Public Policy, April 2000, Volume 3, Number 2.

4. Stanley K. Henshaw, & Kathryn Kost, "Trends in the Characteristics of Women Obtaining Abortions, 1974 to 2004" published by the Guttmacher Institute and available at http://www.guttmacher.org/pubs/2008/09/18/Report_Trends_Women_Obtaining_Abortions.pdf . This report has the best line charts I have seen online to show the trends.

5. Rachel K. Jones, Mia R. S. Zolna, Stanley K. Henshaw & Lawrence B. Finer. "Abortion in the United States: incidence and access to services, 2005, *Perspectives on Sexual and Reproductive Health,* 2008, 40(1):6–16. Text at http://www.guttmacher.org/pubs/psrh/full/4000608.pdf

6. Michael J. New, "Analyzing the Effect of State Legislation on the Incidence of Abortion Among Minors," February 5, 2007, The Heritage Foundation.

7. "State Facts about Abortion: Maryland." Guttmacher Institute. Text and chart at http://www.guttmacher.org/pubs/sfaa/maryland.html

8. Joseph Wright and Michael Bailey, "Reducing Abortion in America: The Effect of Economic and Social Supports." August 2008, Catholics in Alliance for the Common Good.

OTHER BOOKS OF INTEREST

Also from the Feminism & Nonviolence Studies Association:
[For latest updates, see www.fnsa.org]

ProLife Feminism: Yesterday and Today
Edited by Mary Krane Derr, Rachel M. MacNair, and Linda Naranjo-Huebl

Is abortion on "demand" a woman's right, or a wrong inflicted on women? Is it a mark of liberation, or a sign that women are not yet free? From Anglo-Irish writer Mary Wollstonecraft to Kenyan environmentalist and 2004 Nobel Peace Prize laureate Wangari Maathai, many eighteenth- through twenty-first-century feminists have opposed it as violence against fetal lives arising from violence against female lives. This more inclusive, surprisingly old-but-new vision of reproductive choice is called *prolife feminism.*

This book offers brilliant essays on abortion and related social justice issues by the likes of suffragists Susan B. Anthony and Elizabeth Cady Stanton and civil rights leader Fannie Lou Hamer. It not only documents the continuing evolution of prolife feminism worldwide, but more accurately represents the rich diversity of past and present women ☒ and men ☒ who have stood up for both mother and child. It thus is a vital, unique resource for peacemaking in the increasingly globalized abortion war.

Feminism & Nonviolence Studies
www.fnsa.org

Scholarly articles on prolife feminism and the consistent life ethic are on-line, with the 1995 journal volume also available in paper.

Other books by author Rachel M. MacNair:
[For latest updates, see www.rachelmacnair.com/books or
www.rachelmacnair.com/prolifebooks]

Consistently Opposing Killing: From Abortion to Assisted Suicide, the Death Penalty, and War
co-edited with Stephen Zunes
published by Greenwood / Praeger; see www.greenwood.com

This book expands on the consistent life ethic, making the case that issues of violence are connected, solutions are also connected, and there is persuasive power in being consistent by leaving no loopholes in the arguments against violence.

The Psychology of Peace: An Introduction
published by Greenwood / Praeger; see www.greenwood.com

This volume addresses the causes and effects of violence, as well as the causes and effects of behaviors that counter or prevent violence. A brief overview of the central concepts of peace psychology is provided, in addition to study results and questions that still exist. The text includes practical guidance for policymakers, activists, researchers, and all readers who want to better understand this major aspect of the human condition. Intended primarily to support current thinking in the field, many points that are still matters of controversy are identified as such, with alternative views offered where appropriate. While graduate and undergraduate psychology students and scholars will appreciate the text, this book will also enlighten interested readers in the fields of sociology, theology, law, history, and political science.

Perpetration-Induced Traumatic Stress: The Psychological Consequences of Killing
published by Greenwood / Praeger; see www.greenwood.com

This volume introduces the concept of Perpetration-Induced Traumatic Stress (PITS), a form of PTSD symptoms caused not by traditionally expected roles, such as being a victim or rescuer in trauma, but by being an active participant in causing trauma. Sufferers of PITS may be in the roles of soldiers, executioners, or police officers, where it is socially acceptable or even expected for them to cause trauma, including death. Scattered evidence of PITS is consolidated, its implications are explored, and exciting potentials for future research are suggested. Compared to the more widely understood PTSD, there appears to be greater severity and different symptom patterns for those affected by PITS. Obvious differences to be explored for those who kill include questions of context, guilt, meaning, content of dreams, and sociological questions, leading to special implications for therapy, research into the causality of PTSD, and violence prevention efforts. Disciplines including sociology, public policy, history, philosophy, and theology will also find applications for this groundbreaking material.

Working for Peace: A Handbook of Practical Psychology
Rachel M. MacNair, Editor, with Psychologists for Social Responsibility
published by Impact Publishers; see www.impactpublishers.com/books/Working_for_Peace.html

The most complete guidebook yet to social activism. Forty active peace workers -- psychologists, social workers, communication specialists and other professionals -- offer detailed practical guidance on getting yourself together, maintaining an effective group of volunteers, and getting the word out to the larger community.

Thirty-two information-packed chapters include: Cultivating Inner Peace; Overcoming Anger and Anxiety; Overcoming Helplessness and Discouragement; Overcoming Burnout; Motivating Others; Effective Group Meetings and Decision Making; Using Conflict Creatively;

Promoting Peaceful Interaction; Nonviolent Communication; Conflict Transformation Skills; From Anger to Peace; Preparing for Nonviolent Confrontations; Effective Media Communication; Techniques of Behavior Change; Humor for Peace.

Gaining Mind of Peace: Why Violence Happens and How to Stop It
published by Xlibris; see www.xlibris.com/GainingMindofPeace

This is explaining the psychology of peace, young people's version.

Why are there wars? Why do people destroy with terrorism, riots, lynchings? Why do they bully others, or look away when others are in trouble? People who study the mind and behavior -- psychologists -- have been trying to figure this out for a long time. This book explains some of what we know so far. It also gives ideas for what we can do about it, especially what young people can do. For grades 6 and up.

History Shows: Winning with Nonviolent Action
published by Xlibris; see www.xlibris.com/HistoryShows

Did you know that large nonviolent campaigns go back at least as far as the ancient Romans, whose workers staged a major walk-out in 494 B. C.? Did you know that several brutal dictatorships and entrenched empires have been toppled by nonviolent movements? Did you know this has been going on throughout history, all over the world, by people of different religions and backgrounds? Even governments have engaged in nonviolence.

This book gives short stories of some of the major nonviolent actions that have succeeded. Each page has separate cases, so pages can be photocopied for history or other social studies classes to enrich understanding of different peoples and times. Young people can learn about the part of history that war-focused texts tend to overlook. Adults can be educated with an overview of the broad span of how well nonviolent action has worked in the past. Both can learn the basics of the history of nonviolent action.

Web pages which the author coordinates:

www.rachelmacnair.com/pits – explains the psychological consequences of killing, and links to other parts of the web page with personal stories, examples from world literature, and an updated bibliography

www.prolifequakers.org – site of the Friends Witness for a Pro-life Peace Testimony, pro-life group for the Religious Society of Friends (Quakers).

Web pages for pro-life feminism and/or the consistent life ethic include:

Consistent Life: An International Network for Peace & Life
www.consistent-life.org

Institute for Integrated Social Analysis, research arm of Consistent Life
http://www.consistent-life.org/research.html

Feminists for Life of America
www.feministsforlife.org

Feminists Choosing Life
www.feministschoosinglife.org

Nonviolent Choice Directory
www.nonviolentchoice.info
www.nonviolentchoice.blogspot.com

No Violence, Period
http://swissnet.ai.mit.edu/~rauch/nvp/articles.html

Index

www.ingramcontent.com/pod-product-compliance
Lightning Source LLC
Chambersburg PA
CBHW060623290526
45793CB00001B/121